ReMixology

*Classic Cocktails,
Reconsidered and Reinvented*

ReMixology

Classic Cocktails, Reconsidered and Reinvented

Michael Turback & Julia Hastings-Black

Skyhorse Publishing

DEDICATION

To David Augustus Embury, whose classic 1948 work, *The Fine Art of Mixing Drinks*, offers this observation:

"The well-made cocktail is one of the most gracious of drinks. It pleases the senses. The shared delight of those who partake in common of this refreshing nectar breaks the ice of formal reserve. Taut nerves relax, taut muscles relax, tired eyes brighten, tongues loosen, friendships deepen—the whole world becomes a better place in which to live."

CONTENTS

APÉRITIF

*"The framework of a cocktail recipe has a formula
just like a sheet of music. You can take this formula
and play it in one key, but it will also work
if you play it in a higher or lower key."*

—Mixologist Tony Conigliaro

America is the land of reinvention, and the cocktail has always been a way to reinvent old, established spirits, to make drinking more civilized. Even in the current wave of progressive mixology, bartenders and drinkers are renewing their appreciation for classic cocktails—sophisticated intoxicants that have withstood the test of time, as each successive generation has found them as pleasurable as the one before. Yet history tells us that once a cocktail achieved prominence at the bar, the impulse to invent variations was irresistible.

Offered for your consideration are the vanguard of cocktails, drinks of choice which have achieved popular favor over a long period of time: Manhattan, Martini, Whiskey Sour, Alexander, Daiquiri, Old Fashioned, Negroni, Champagne Cocktail, Bloody Mary, and Irish Coffee. Collectively, they provide the foundation upon which most other cocktails are based.

The value of history lies in what is learned from the past, and, in the midst of a worldwide cocktail renaissance, the new generation of freethinking mixologists has been reimagining the classics in wonderful ways, introducing flavors and ingredients in an in-depth exploration of new and deeper, more complex tasting experiences. While you might think that tinkering with their formulas would be somewhat like drawing a moustache on the Mona Lisa, quite the contrary. It is precisely because of their timeless appeal that so many bartenders find them ideal jumping-off points in the quest for each drink's true potential.

Mixology is an art—nurtured by spirit, flavor, aroma, color, and imagination. For the drinkmaker, original recipes serve as the touchstones of cocktailing, and as long as one follows the rules, it's hard to make a bad one. Yet it's the mark of the great cocktail to be able to spawn not only artisanal makeovers but also variations on the variations.

To illustrate the link between past and present, we're about to reexamine these ten classics—each one highlighting the most engaging qualities in a base spirit—along a time- and field-tested path to transformation behind the bar, grounded in history and elevated by fresh ingredients and a sense of fun.

TOOLS OF THE TRADE

Boston Shaker

Dating all the way back to late nineteenth century "Beantown," the Boston shaker has been a fundamental bar tool, and it remains the professional standard, pure and simple. The two-piece shaker consists of a stainless steel cup and mixing glass; the glass is used alone for stirring drinks with ice, and the two pieces are joined together for shaking ingredients with the cup fitting over the glass, creating a seal when gently tapped into place. (When making two drinks at once, use less ice to make room in the shaker.)

TIP: *Shaking technique should result in a drink that's cold yet undiluted, simultaneously blended and aerated. In* The Thin Man, *William Powell instructs his bartender on the art of shaking: "The important thing is the rhythm. Always have rhythm in your shaking. Now a Manhattan you always shake to foxtrot time, a Bronx to two-step time, a dry Martini you always shake to waltz time."*

Hawthorne Strainer

The all-purpose strainer is a paddle-like, perforated metal device with a continuous coil of wire around its perimeter, ensuring a spill-proof fit, compatible with the Boston shaker. For drinks that are shaken or stirred with ice and served neat or over new ice, the strainer is used to separate ice from the liquid.

TIP: *Place your index finger over the handle to hold it firmly in place and strain the drink into the serving glass. To get the last drop, give the shaker a sharp twist as you return it to an upright position.*

Fine-Mesh Strainer

Pouring from a Boston shaker with a Hawthorne strainer through a tea strainer or a fine mesh strainer is known as "double straining." This secondary filter removes smaller particles, froth, pulp, seeds, and other unwanted ingredients, ensuring a clean, clear drink.

TIP: This tool is indispensable when straining cocktails with herbs, such as mint or basil.

Jigger and Pony

Ingredients in proper cocktails must be measured to the fraction of an ounce. A stainless steel instrument with two opposing cones in an hourglass shape is recommended for precise, consistent calibration of liquids in the preparation of cocktails. The larger cone (jigger) typically holds 1½ ounces while the smaller cone (pony) holds ¾ ounce. With no need for the guesswork of free-pouring, cocktails will honor the recipe a skilled bartender labored to create. (In countries that use the metric system, the measures are usually 40 ml and 20 ml.)

TIP: Charles H. Baker Jr. calls cocktail mixing "an exacting chemical art." Consider purchasing other jiggers for more specific measurements. Single jiggers come in iterations from a quarter of an ounce to two ounces.

Bar Spoon

Certain cocktails, particularly those made with spirits only, should always be stirred, chilling the drink without the undue aeration of shaking. Essential to stirring, the metal, long-handled bar spoon (for reaching the bottom of tall glasses) has a spiral handle (for easy twisting of the shaft) used to agitate or twirl ice through the ingredients and a spoon used for a teaspoon measure.

TIP: Hold the twisted shaft of the bar spoon between your thumb and first two fingers. Dunk the bar spoon into the glass and twirl the shaft back and forth and up and down in a fluid motion for 10 to 20 seconds to achieve the desired temperature.

Muddler

Similar to a pestle, the muddler is a blunt instrument used to mash and agitate herbs, fruits, or other solid ingredients in the bottom of a mixing glass, extracting flavors and aromatics. Most commonly made of hardwood, the muddler should be artfully weighted and teardrop-shaped, with a diameter of about 1½ inches at the widest point and long enough to reach the bottom of mixing glasses.

TIP: When muddling herbs to release essential oils, be gentle, avoiding the release of bitterness from the stems. For muddling fruit such as strawberries, cutting into small pieces makes them easier to work with.

Ice / Ice Tray

Oversize ice cubes help maintain the integrity of cocktails. A larger, thicker surface melts slower, so drinks stay colder longer and don't get watered down. Use larger molds to freeze distilled, purified, natural spring or bottled water, and keep the ice fresh by rotating in and out of the freezer.

TIP: A good drink is very cold. To pre-chill, fill glasses to the brim with ice and water (soda water works best) and let them sit while you mix the drinks. Just before pouring drinks, discard the contents of each glass.

Bar Knives

Adding a garnish of citrus zest, twist, or peel "medallion" provides the finishing touch to many cocktails. A sharp paring knife and cutting board are basic requirements. In addition, the zester/channel knife combo uses small circular holes to zest the aromatic peel of citrus fruits (without grating into the bitter pith) and a blade that cuts ¼-inch wide strips of rind for spirals.

TIP: To liberate the wonderfully aromatic spray of essential oil over a drink, hold the peel horizontally about one inch above the surface, outer skin side facing downward. Gently but firmly twist one end clockwise and the other counterclockwise. Rub the outside of the peel around the rim of the glass so that any remaining oils adhere to the rim and drop into the drink.

Citrus Juicer

Always use fresh-squeezed lemons, limes, or oranges for more aromatic and fresher-tasting drinks. The hand-press citrus juicer provides small amounts of juice with minimal effort. Simply insert the halved fruit into the bowl of the squeezer and press down, using the top part to push the juice through the strainer. The bowl juicer is another way to easily juice citrus fruits and store small amounts of juice before adding it to a recipe.

TIP: *To get the most juice yield out of your citrus, use fruits at room temperature. Roll the fruit with your palm on the kitchen countertop a few times before you juice.*

Glassware

The proper glass for a cocktail may also be considered a tool. Glassware is available in a wide range of styles, sizes, and decorative motifs, and while fashion and presentation can heighten the imbibing experience, more basic criteria should be contemplated. Ideal for a straight-up cocktail, the shallow, curvaceous coupe encourages one to sip a drink rather than tossing it back in large gulps, and its stem allows a drinker to hold the glass without affecting the temperature; the wide bowl places the surface of the drink directly under the drinker's nose, ensuring that the aromatic element has the desired effect.

TIP: *The coupe started life as a champagne glass, later adapted to holding cocktails in swanky, post-Prohibition nightclubs during the 1930s and '40s. The coupe is in vogue once again, both for its versatility as well as homage to the heyday of cocktail culture.*

Making Simple Syrup

Many cocktail recipes call for simple syrup (or bar syrup) as a sweetener, often used to balance citric acid. The most typical "recipe" couldn't be easier to execute: add one cup water into a pan, bring to a boil, then stir in 1½ cups (or up to 2 cups) of plain granulated sugar. Turn the heat to low, and stir continually until the sugar dissolves completely. Allow the syrup to cool to room temperature, then pour into a clean glass jar and store in the refrigerator.

ALEXANDER

Mother of all cream drinks, the Alexander first appeared at Rector's, the legendary New York City lobster palace in 1900. Officials of the Delaware, Lackawanna, and Western Railroad had arranged for a dinner party at the restaurant to celebrate their new ad campaign, featuring a fictitious character named "Phoebe Snow," pictured in a white dress to promote the company's clean-burning locomotives. Rector's head bartender, Troy Alexander, concocted a "snow-white" cocktail for the occasion, a drink which now bears his name. In *The Gun Club Drink Book* (1939), author Charles Browne explained the popularity of cream drinks during and immediately after Prohibition: "During the short but rather bizarre reconstruction period, the youth of the nation weaned themselves by drinking so-called cocktails containing milk or cream, and such drinks as 'Alexander's cocktail' were in vogue."

Alexander, circa 1915

Back in the days before Prohibition, the Alexander had become a staple at the American bar. Grover Cleveland Alexander pitched the Philadelphia Phillies to victory over Boston in the opening game of the 1915 World Series, and the city's Racquet Club celebrated by serving Alexander cocktails throughout the series. According to Hugo Ensslin in *Recipes for Mixed Drinks*, published in the same year, all three ingredients were to be combined in equal measure.

1 ounce Gin
1 ounce White Crème de Cacao
1 ounce fresh Cream

Combine ingredients in a mixing glass with cracked ice. Shake vigorously and strain into chilled cocktail coupe glass.

Brandy Alexander

First known as the Alexander #2, with brandy replacing gin and dark crème de cacao replacing white, the drink was first served in 1922 at the Royal Wedding of Princess Mary of the British Royal Family and Henry Charles George, the Viscount Lascelles, one of several brandy-based cocktails which originated in Europe during American Prohibition. According to *The Cocktail Guide and Ladies' Companion*, in some circles, the drink was called a Panama Hattie.

1½ ounces Brandy
1 ounce Dark Crème de Cacao
1 ounce fresh Cream

Combine ingredients in a mixing glass with cracked ice. Shake vigorously and strain into chilled cocktail coupe glass.

Alexander's Sister

In 1885, Emile Giffard, a pharmacist in Angers, France, invented a pure, clear, and refined white mint liqueur for guests of the Grand Hotel, offering relief from a particularly hot summer. Crème de menthe, in both white and green, became a popular liqueur and an ingredient in cocktail recipes, among them a sibling to the Alexander. In *The Savoy Cocktail Book*, published in London in 1930, Harry Craddock warned that "Ladies are advised to avoid this cocktail as often as possible."

1 ounce Gin
1 ounce Green Crème de Menthe
1 ounce fresh Cream

Combine ingredients in a mixing glass with cracked ice. Shake vigorously and strain into chilled cocktail coupe glass.

Grasshopper

This mint-green, cream-based libation was reportedly invented pre-Prohibition in a 1919 New York City cocktail contest for which Philbert Guichet, owner of Tujague's (the second oldest restaurant in New Orleans), took home second place. Guichet proudly brought the drink—supposedly named for its bright green color—back to New Orleans where it caught on as a dessert cocktail.

1 ounce Green Crème de Menthe
1 ounce White Crème de Cacao
1 ounce fresh Cream
1 dash Cognac (optional)

Combine ingredients in a mixing glass with cracked ice. Shake vigorously and strain into chilled cocktail coupe glass. Add a dash of cognac over the top.

Café de Paris

In 1912, Vernon and Irene Castle, who popularized modern ballroom dancing in America, made their debut at the Café de Paris, located at the corner of Forty-Second Street and Seventh Avenue in the heart of New York's Times Square. A namesake cocktail was immortalized in Harry McElhone's *Barflies and Cocktails* (1927).

1½ ounces Gin
1 teaspoon Anisette
1 teaspoon fresh Cream
1 Egg White

Combine ingredients in a mixing glass with cracked ice. Shake vigorously and strain into chilled cocktail coupe glass.

The Old Waldorf's Last

According to Charles H. Baker, Jr. in the 1939 *Gentleman's Companion*, this was the last original cocktail to come from the legendary Men's Bar at the Waldorf Hotel (Fifth Avenue and Thirty-Fourth Street), "where titanic, two-fisted Wall Streeters and important folk from all over the world used to stand six or eight deep before mahogany."

1½ ounces Gin
1½ ounces Orange Curaçao
1½ ounces fresh Cream

Combine ingredients in a mixing glass with cracked ice. Shake vigorously and strain into chilled cocktail coupe glass.

Vanishing Cream

Crosby Gaige, once described as "Manhattan's authentically distinguished man-about-the-boulevards," recommended the addition of a cherry to this 1940s-era cream drink. "Never argue with a cherry or strike it in anger," cautioned Gaige.

2 ounces Apricot Brandy
1 ounce fresh Cream
1 dash Gin
Maraschino Cherry

Combine ingredients in a mixing glass with cracked ice. Shake vigorously and strain into chilled cocktail coupe glass. Drop cherry into the glass.

Alexander the Great

Nelson Eddy co-starred with Jeanette MacDonald in eight films in the 1930s and '40s. In *The Stork Club Bar Book*, Lucius Beebe writes, "An improvement, as some may think, on the conventional Alexander cocktail is the brainstorm child of Nelson Eddy and he calls it 'Alexander the Great.' Shake until cold as Siberia. Watch your Steppes, because more than three of these gives the consumer a wolfish appetite."

½ ounce White Crème de Cacao
½ ounce Coffee Liqueur
½ ounce fresh Cream
1½ ounces Vodka

Combine ingredients in a mixing glass with cracked ice. Shake vigorously and strain into chilled cocktail coupe glass.

Whizz-Doodle

As the bartender of New York's Ashland House for forty years, Patrick Gavin Duffy served drinks to the likes of Mark Twain, Oscar Wilde, and J.P. Morgan. In 1948, he chronicled their favorite tipples in his well-regarded tome, *The Official Mixer's Manual*. Silly cocktail names among the offerings included the Why Not, Everything But, and Whizz-Doodle.

¾ ounce Scotch Whisky
¾ ounce fresh Cream
¾ ounce White Crème de Cacao
¾ ounce Gin

Combine ingredients in a mixing glass with cracked ice. Shake vigorously and strain into chilled cocktail coupe glass.

Pink Squirrel

Bryant Sharp opened a beer hall in Milwaukee in 1936, and two years later decided to give up beer in favor of cocktails. As part of this transformation, he took out the jukebox and replaced it with a record player, serenading customers with classical music. It was the first cocktail lounge in Wisconsin and the birthplace of the creamy, nutty-flavored Pink Squirrel.

1 ounce Crème de Noyaux
1 ounce White Crème de Cacao
1 ounce fresh Cream

Combine ingredients in a mixing glass with cracked ice. Shake vigorously and strain into chilled cocktail coupe glass.

White Russian

Although the Black Russian (vodka and coffee liqueur) dates back to 1949, dairy didn't enter the picture until 1961 when *The Diners' Club Drink Book* featured a recipe that added cream to the mix. The White Russian cocktail was later immortalized by Jeff Bridges' character, "the Dude," the protagonist of cult classic *The Big Lebowski*. In the film, the Dude refers to the drink as a "Caucasian." (A Dirty Russian is made with chocolate milk instead of cream; the Toasted Almond substitutes Amaretto for Vodka; a Mudslide replaces fresh cream with Bailey's Irish Cream).

2 ounces Vodka
1 ounce Kahlúa (or other Coffee Liqueur)
1 ounce fresh Cream

Combine vodka and coffee liqueur in a rocks glass filled with ice. Stir. Float cream by holding a teaspoon bottom-side up over the glass and pouring the cream slowly over it.

Golden Cadillac

Originally produced in Livorno, Italy, in 1896, Galliano first became popular outside Europe after World War II as American soldiers brought it home. Galliano's sweet vanilla-anise is the key flavor in the Golden Cadillac, a "disco era" drink created at Poor Red's Bar-B-Q in El Dorado, California. (The now-defunct bar also devised the Brown Cow Cocktail, a coffee liqueur and milk combo).

¾ ounce fresh Cream
¾ ounce White Crème de Cacao
¾ ounce Galliano

Combine ingredients in a mixing glass with cracked ice. Shake vigorously and strain into chilled cocktail coupe glass.

Chai Alexander

At Philadelphia's Rex 1515, guests sip on an opulent, cognac-spiked version of the Alexander, mixed to a frothy finish by Heather Rodkey. More than simply a dessert accompaniment, the interplay of flavors and textures becomes a potential replacement for the after-dinner course altogether.

2 ounces Salignac Cognac
1 ounce RumChata Cream Liqueur
1 ounce White Crème de Cacao
2 dashes Chocolate Bitters
Grated Nutmeg, for garnish
Brandied Cherry, for garnish

Combine ingredients in a mixing glass with cracked ice. Shake vigorously and strain into chilled Martini glass. Garnish with a pinch of nutmeg and brandied cherry on a bamboo skewer.

La Cavalletta

What better cocktail to serve postprandial than something which combines the nightcap role of an Alexander with the digestif properties of Fernet Branca. Fashionable in the bars of northern Italy, this version (in Italian, *cavalletta* means "grasshopper") calls for Branca Menta, the cool, fresh, minty cousin of the bracing original, adding an almost candy cane–like flavor to the creamy base.

1 ounce Branca Menta
1 ounce Crème de Cacao
1 ounce fresh Cream
Grated Nutmeg, for garnish

Combine ingredients in a mixing glass with cracked ice. Shake vigorously and strain into a rocks glass. Garnish with dusting of nutmeg.

The Bushwacker

The Bushwacker is a regionally popular cocktail made of rum, coffee and chocolate liqueurs, and vanilla ice cream, said to have been invented by Linda Murphy in 1975, the owner of the Sandshaker Beach Bar in Pensacola Beach, Florida. Locals along coastal Florida and Alabama sometimes add a 151-proof rum topper for extra kick.

1 ounce Dark Rum
1 ounce Kahlúa
1 ounce Dark Crème de Cacao
2 ounces Cream of Coconut

1 scoop Vanilla Ice Cream
1 cup ice
Grated Nutmeg, for garnish

Blend all the ingredients together with cracked ice in a blender. Pour into a hurricane glass and dust the surface with nutmeg. (Whipped cream and maraschino cherry are additional options for garnish.)

Irish Girl Scout

The foundation of the chocolaty, minty, drinkable dessert from the Irish Inn in Glen Echo, Maryland is vodka from Ireland, named for the legendary king Brian Boru, who united the Emerald Isle in 1014. Inspired by those irresistible Thin Mint Girl Scout cookies, the sipping experience is enhanced with a cookie-rimmed glass.

1 ounce Boru Vodka
½ ounce White Creme de Cacao
½ ounce Green Creme de Menthe
1 ounce Half and Half
Oreo Cookie Crumbs, for garnish*

Combine ingredients in a mixing glass with cracked ice and shake vigorously. Strain into the prepared martini glass.

*Oreo Cookie Crumb Garnish: Spread simple syrup on a plate, and dip the rim of a chilled martini glass into it to lightly coat the rim. Spread crumbled cookies on another plate, and dip the coated rim into the crumbs to adhere.

Flying Grasshopper

Memoirs Restaurant in Colchester, the oldest town in Britain, is ensconced in an ornate former library with vaulted ceilings, where handcrafted cocktails include a sweet, creamy, decadent version of a blended Grasshopper which Brits shamelessly refer to as a gender appropriate "girly" drink, eclipsing the cocktail that inspired it.

½ ounce Vodka
½ ounce Green Crème de Menthe
½ ounce White Crème de Cacao
1 scoop Vanilla Ice Cream

½ ounce Heavy Cream
Cinnamon Powder, for garnish
Mint Leaf, for garnish
Cinnamon Stick, for garnish

Purée ice cream, vodka, crème de menthe, crème de cacao, and heavy cream in a blender; pour into a chilled martini glass. Garnish with a dusting of cinnamon, a mint leaf to one side, and place cinnamon stick on top to float.

Hazelnut Alexander

Its familiar bottle resembles the habit of a Franciscan friar. The hazelnut flavor of Frangelico liqueur puts a toasty spin on the classic Alexander, brainstorm of the bar team at Sam's of Cornwall, England. The fruitiness of cognac provides the ideal base for the rich, nutty flavor, complementing creamy notes of chocolate and vanilla. An indulgent, dessert-like drink.

¾ ounce Courvoisier
¾ ounce Frangelico
¾ ounce White Crème de Cacao
¾ ounce fresh Cream

Combine ingredients in a mixing glass with cracked ice. Shake vigorously and strain into chilled cocktail coupe glass.

Bettina Alexander

This tropical-inspired version of the Alexander, from the imagination of mixologist Bettina Reece of the West Side Lounge in Cambridge, Massachusetts, downplays the brandy, mixes rum in place of crème de cacao, and substitutes the silky mouthfeel of coconut milk for cream. Close your eyes and sip on her eponymous cocktail—you can pretend you're on an island in the Caribbean.

1½ ounces Bully Boy Rum
½ ounce Brandy
½ ounce Simple Syrup
1 ounce Coconut Milk
Grated Nutmeg, for garnish

Combine ingredients in a mixing glass with cracked ice. Shake vigorously and strain into a rocks glass. Garnish with dusting of nutmeg.

~~~~~~

Bourbon Grasshopper

In the Midwest, the quintessential Grasshopper is a blended dessert drink, squarely in the "guilty pleasure" category among a certain subset of drinkers. At Bonfyre American Grille in Madison, Wisconsin, mixologist Manuel Barrales's version is a glorified milkshake that substitutes ice cream for regular cream and adds a shot of Bourbon for grown-ups. (For a more demure, sage-green version, use chocolate-hued dark crème de cacao).

1 ounce Bourbon
2 scoops Vanilla Ice Cream
¼ ounce White Créme de Cacao
¾ ounce Green Créme de Menthe + extra for garnish
Whipped Cream, for garnish

Purée ice cream, bourbon, crème de menthe, and crème de cacao in a blender; pour into a cocktail glass. Top with a dollop of whipped cream; drizzle crème de menthe over top.

Staycation

You know what they say—the world is a better place with bacon in it. New York's Sugar and Plumm uses a process of infusing the bourbon called "fat washing." You're only going to be using the bacon fat, so save the bacon for later. (A bacon with more smokiness creates a better and more sophisticated drink). With ice cream and chocolate syrup, the Staycation morphs into an honest-to-goodness dessert.

2 ounces Bacon-Infused Bourbon*
2 scoops Vanilla Ice Cream
1 ounce Cold-Brew Coffee
½ ounce Hershey's Chocolate Syrup
Whipped Cream, for garnish
Toasted Coconut, for garnish
Chocolate Bark, for garnish

Combine ingredients in a blender and blend until smooth. Pour into a cocktail glass lined with chocolate syrup. Top with whipped cream, toasted coconut, and chocolate bark. Serve with large straw.

*Bacon-Infused Bourbon: Cook 3 to 4 strips of bacon in pan and reserve rendered fat. When bacon fat has cooled, pour off one ounce from pan. Pour 750 ml of bourbon into a non-porous container. Strain the bacon fat into the container and infuse for 4 to 6 hours at room temperature. Place mixture in freezer until all the fat is solidified. With a slotted spoon, remove fat and strain infused Bourbon back into bottle.

Caribbean Milk Punch

It was New Orleans restaurateur Ella Brennan who invented brunch, and among eye-opener cocktails at legendary Brennan's in the French Quarter of New Orleans is beverage director Drew Brandwein's rich, boozy version of a punch that holds a place of honor in the city's drink pantheon—alongside the Sazerac and the Ramos Gin Fizz. The taste of alcohol is cleverly masked by the creamy sweetness, so exercise caution and clear your calendar for the afternoon.

1 ounce Smith & Cross Jamaica Rum
½ ounce Maker's Mark Bourbon
1 ounce Vanilla Bean-infused Simple Syrup
1 ounce Heavy Cream
Grated Nutmeg, for garnish

Combine ingredients in a mixing glass with cracked ice. Shake vigorously until frothy and strain into a chilled cocktail coupe glass. Dust with grated nutmeg.

BLOODY MARY

"Meet me down in the bar," entreated W. C. Fields. "We'll drink break-fast together." The origination of the only drink that's socially accept-able to drink in the morning links back to comedian, songwriter, and movie producer George Jessel, who, beginning in 1927, mixed half-vodka and half-tomato juice to help with his morning hangovers from the night before. In his words: "the juice for body and the vodka for spirit." During the 1930s, bartender Henry Zbikiewicz was charged with mixing Jessel's drink at the '21' Club, and *New York Herald* gossip columnist Lucius Beebe took note, citing "George Jessel's Pick-Me-Up." The restorative was later embellished and perfected by Fernand Petiot at Harry's New York Bar in Paris. "Jessel said he created it," explained Petiot, "but it was really nothing but vodka and tomato juice when I took it over."

Red Snapper

Upon the repeal of Prohibition, Vincent Astor hired Fernand Petiot to run the bar at his New York hotel, the St. Regis, overlooking Fifth Avenue. It was at the King Cole Bar where Petiot, the drink's true architect, served America's first Bloody Mary to Sergei "Serge" Obolensky, the exiled Russian prince who became publicity director for Hilton Hotels. Since "Bloody Mary" was deemed too vulgar a name for the swanky St. Regis, the drink was renamed "Red Snapper" to make it sound a bit less déclassé.

1 ounce Vodka
2 ounces Tomato juice
1 dash Lemon Juice
2 dashes Salt

2 dashes Black Pepper
2 dashes Cayenne Pepper
3 dashes Worcestershire
Lemon wedge, for garnish

Combine ingredients in a mixing glass with cracked ice. Shake vigorously and strain into a tall cocktail glass. Garnish with lemon.

Bloody Bull

A Bloody Mary–like sipper that swaps meaty broth for tomato juice was apparently thought up at Detroit's Caucus Club around 1952 and called the "Bull Shot." Not to be outdone, the white-coated technicians behind the bar at Brennan's Restaurant in New Orleans put back the tomato juice along with the beef broth for a drink to accompany "Breakfast at Brennan's," a longstanding French Quarter tradition.

1½ ounces Vodka
1½ ounces Campbell's Beef Broth
1½ ounces Tomato Juice
2 dashes Worcestershire

2 dashes Celery Salt
1 dash Tabasco
1 pinch Black Pepper
Lime wedge, for garnish.

Combine ingredients in a 10-ounce highball glass with ice. Stir to combine. Garnish with lime.

Butch's Jumbo Bloody Mary

A crunchy stalk of palate-cooling celery has become the Bloody Mary's mainstay garnish, and for that we are in debt to a wacky Chicago bar. It was at Butch McGuire's in 1961 where a bartender first offered a stalk of celery to an impatient, hangover-nursing patron who couldn't wait for a swizzle stick to stir his drink. We've come to rely on a bite of astringent celery between sips, cutting through palate-coating tomato juice to moderate the intensity of salt and heat.

2 ounces Vodka
2 dashes Worcestershire Sauce
3 turns of a pepper grinder filled with
    Black Peppercorns
2 ounces Stu's Bloody Mary Concentrate

6 ounces Tomato Juice
1 dash Tabasco (optional)
½ teaspoon Horseradish Sauce (optional)
1 Lime wedge, for garnish
1 leafy Celery stalk, for garnish

Combine ingredients in a large glass mug with ice. Stir to combine. Garnish with lime and celery.

Bloody Caesar

In 1969, tasked with creating a signature drink for the Calgary Inn's new Italian restaurant in Calgary, Alberta, Canada, Walter Chell mixed vodka with clam and tomato juice, Worcestershire sauce, and other spices, creating a "Canadian Bloody Mary." According to Chell, his inspiration came from Spaghetti alle Vongole, a dish of spaghetti with tomato sauce and clams. (A variation with Irish whiskey in place of vodka is called a Red Devil.)

1 tablespoon Celery Salt
½ tablespoon Black Pepper
1 Lime wedge + 1 additional for garnish
1 ounce Vodka
½ teaspoon Worcestershire

½ teaspoon Tabasco
Clamato Juice (or a mix of 2 parts clam juice to
    1 part tomato juice)
Celery stick, for garnish

Spread the mix of celery salt and black pepper on a small plate. Rub the rim of a tall glass with the lime wedge, and dip rim in the spice mix. Add cracked ice to the glass; set aside. Combine vodka, Worchestershire, tabasco, and clamato juice in a mixing glass with cracked ice. Stir to combine and strain into reserved glass. Garnish with lime and celery.

Red Eye

"Hair of the dog" refers to an alcoholic beverage consumed as a hangover remedy, short for "hair of the dog that bit you," meaning the best cure for what ails you is to have some more of it. The Mexican beer-and-tomato juice "Michelada" is likely the inspiration for this drink, popularized in the 1988 film *Cocktail* (with a young Tom Cruise as bartender).

6 ounces Tomato Juice, chilled
12 ounces Beer
1 raw Egg

Pour tomato juice into a large frosted mug. Over tomato juice, pour cold beer. Do not stir. Crack egg, drop contents into mug. Do not stir. Discard eggshell.

Green Eye-Opener

Shamelessly high-end, New York's Sign of the Dove was known for its lush interior, with gas lamps, skylights, Venetian glass, discreetly arranged tables, and tasteful floral arrangements—and for a Bloody Mary–inspired yet tomato-less drink served at brunch. Sign of the Dove closed in 1998, but the signature cocktail lives on.

1 dash Blue Curaçao
1 dash Cointreau
1½ ounces Vodka
1 dash Rose's Lime Juice

2 ounces Orange Juice
Celery Salt, to taste
Salt and Black Pepper, to taste
Celery stalk, for garnish

Combine Blue Curaçao, Cointreau, vodka, Rose's lime juice, orange juice, and celery salt in a tall, ice-filled glass. Add salt and pepper to taste. Stir with celery stalk.

Blood Transfusion

Esteemed mixologist Salvatore Calabrese created this post-binge restorer at the Library Bar of the Lanesborough Hotel in London. According to Calabrese, "It addresses the stomach first (through the Fernet Branca), then the headache, then the general malaise in the body—the combination will either cure you or finish you off."

1 ounce Vodka
1 ounce Sherry
5 ounces Tomato Juice
1 ounce Lime Juice, freshly squeezed

Pinch of Celery Salt
2 dashes Worcestershire
2 thin slices fresh Chile Pepper
1 ounce Fernet Branca

Combine all ingredients (except Fernet Branca) in a mixing glass with cracked ice. Shake vigorously, and strain into a highball glass filled with fresh ice. Top with a float of Fernet Branca.

Hail Mary

In American football, a long forward pass that requires divine intervention for a successful completion is called a "Hail Mary," the name appropriated by Brendan Dorr at B&O American Brasserie in support of his hometown Baltimore Ravens. It's kind of an "Unbloody" Mary, as lemon and pomegranate juices replace time-honored tomato with the intense flavor of cassis in place of spices.

1¼ ounces Hangar One Mandarin Blossom Vodka
½ ounce Torani Cassis Syrup
¾ ounce Lemon Juice, freshly squeezed
¾ ounce Pomegranate Juice
Lemon peel, for garnish

Combine ingredients in a mixing glass with cracked ice. Shake vigorously, and strain into a chilled cocktail glass. Express lemon peel over the glass, rub it around the rim, and drop it in.

Bloody Maria

Named for two nineteenth-century racehorses, Saxon + Parole is a kind of bluegrass men's club in New York City's NoHo neighborhood, where cocktail artisans mix up this Mexican-inspired spin on the Bloody Mary. Laced with both tequila and mezcal, the Bloody Maria gains extra kick from a hefty dose of chipotle pepper purée and is generously adorned with pearl onion, cornichons, and shiny red cherry tomato.

2 tablespoons Sea Salt
Lime wedge
1½ ounces Olmeca Altos Blanco Tequila
¼ ounce Del Maguey Vida Mezcal
½ ounce Lime Juice, freshly squeezed
1 teaspoon Chipotle Peppers, puréed

Bloody Mary Mix*
Pinch of Cilantro
Cherry Tomato, for garnish
Cornichon, for garnish
Pickled Pearl Onion, for garnish

Spread sea salt on a small plate. Rub the rim of a tall glass with the lime wedge, and dip rim in the salt. Add cracked ice to the glass; set aside. Combine tequila, mezcal, lime juice, chipotle purée, and Bloody Mary mix in a mixing glass with cracked ice. Stir to combine and strain into reserved glass. Sprinkle with cilantro, and garnish with skewered cherry tomato, cornichon, and pickled pearl onion.

*Bloody Mary Mix:
1 quart fresh Roma tomatoes, crushed
5 ounces Carrot Juice
6½ ounces Celery Juice
3 ounces Cucumber Juice
3 ounces Red Bell Pepper Purée
1 ounce Lemon Juice

1 teaspoon Tomato Paste
1 teaspoon Maldon Salt
1 teaspoon Celery Salt
1 teaspoon Black Pepper
1 teaspoon Horseradish
1 dash Worcestershire Sauce

The Green Mary

Not all Bloody Marys are bloody. At The Diner in Washington, DC, mixologists switch things up by using a mix of tomatillos and kale, putting an ingenious twist on the classic morning-after cocktail and turning trademark red into green. A vigorous kick of jalapeño-infused vodka rounds out the spicy flavor profile.

2 tablespoons Kosher Salt
Lime wedge
2 ounces Jalapeño-Infused Vodka*
5 ounces Green Mix**
Celery stalk, for garnish

Spread kosher salt on a small plate. Rub the rim of a pint glass with the lime wedge and dip rim in the salt. Add cracked ice to the glass; set aside. Combine infused vodka and Green Mix in a mixing glass with cracked ice. Stir to combine and strain into prepared glass. Garnish with celery stalk.

*Jalapeño-Infused Vodka: Add 1 to 2 jalapeño peppers and a 750 ml bottle of vodka to a clean 1-quart mason jar. Let it sit for 24 hours, shaking periodically. Taste and add more jalapeño (seeds and membrane included if you like it extra hot). Strain and filter back into the bottle.

**Green Mix:
4 cups canned Tomatillos, drained
4 cups loosely packed, chopped Kale (blanched and shocked in ice water)
½ cup chopped Green Onion
1 cup chopped Celery
½ cup Lemon Juice, freshly squeezed
¼ cup green Tabasco
¼ cup Worcestershire
1 teaspoon Salt
1 teaspoon Black Pepper

Blend ingredients in batches, using a food processor. Strain through coarse mesh filter. Shake to combine before using.

Bloody Prejudice

Carrots replace tomatoes to create a bright, slightly sweet take on the Bloody Mary, developed at the glamorous Voodoo Rooms bar on West Register Street in Edinburgh, Scotland. The mix of spices kicks up the heat; dominant, spicy-sweet cumin heightens the natural sweetness of carrots, while the citrus twang of lemon freshens the vegetable's rootiness.

¾ ounce Ketel One Citroen
½ ounce Domaine De Canton
1½ ounces Carrot Juice, freshly juiced
½ ounce Lemon Juice, freshly squeezed
Pinch Bloody Spice Mix*
Pickled Carrot and Onion on skewer, for garnish
Coriander sprig, for garnish

Combine ingredients in a mixing glass with cracked ice. Shake vigorously and fine-strain into chilled cocktail coupe glass. Garnish with pickled carrot and onion and coriander sprig.

*Bloody Spice Mix:
1 pinch Cumin
1 pinch Cayenne Pepper
1 pinch Paprika
1 pinch Black Pepper
1 pinch Salt
1 pinch Nutmeg
1 pinch ground Coriander

Golden Beet Bloody Mary

Chef Jason Cichonski of Ela, the inventive bar and restaurant in Philadelphia's Queen Village neighborhood, prepares beet purée for a brunch Bloody Mary that doubles up on vegetables. A bit sweeter and mellower than their deep red cousins, golden beets add distinctive earthy quality to the tomato-anchored Bloody Mary. Thick citrus wedges are wrung for full-force tang to cut both the spirit and spicy broth.

1½ ounces Vodka
½ teaspoon Black Pepper
1 teaspoon grated Horseradish
1 teaspoon Tabasco
1 teaspoon Salt
1 ounce Worchestershire
4 ounces Tomato Juice

¼ ounce Lemon Juice, freshly squeezed
¼ ounce Lime Juice, freshly squeezed
¼ ounce Olive Brine
1 tablespoon Golden Beet Purée*
Lemon wedge, for garnish
Lime wedge, for garnish
Celery stalk, for garnish

Combine ingredients in a pint glass with ice. Stir to combine. Garnish with lemon and lime wedges and celery stalk.

*Golden Beet Purée:
2 roasted Golden Beets, diced
   into small pieces
1 cup Water
⅛ teaspoon Xantham Gum
¼ cup Distilled Vinegar
¼ cup fresh grated Horseradish

¼ cup V8 Juice
¼ cup Cola
Salt
Pepper
Lime Juice

Combine golden beets with water, xanthan gum, distilled vinegar, fresh grated horseradish, V8 juice, and cola. Purée ingredients. Season with salt, pepper, and lime juice to taste (makes 1 quart).

Bloody Maryland

Bartenders in bowties at the Old Ebbitt Grill, an historic oyster bar in Washington, DC, rim each glass of their Bloody Mary–inspired amalgamation with savory Old Bay seasoning and garnish the cocktail with a jumbo shrimp for a spicy, regional flourish. With a bit of beefy heft, it teeters on the boundary between food and drink.

2 tablespoons Old Bay seasoning
Lime wedge
1½ ounces Absolut Peppar
2 tablespoons Beef Broth
⅓ cup Tomato Juice
½ tablespoon Lemon Juice, freshly squeezed
¼ teaspoon Black Pepper, freshly cracked
1 large boiled and chilled Shrimp, for garnish
1 Celery stalk, for garnish
Lemon wedge, for garnish

Spread Old Bay seasoning on a small plate. Rub the rim of a tall glass with the lime wedge and dip rim in Old Bay. Add cracked ice to the glass; set aside. Combine vodka, beef broth, tomato juice, lemon juice, and black pepper in a mixing glass with cracked ice. Stir to combine, and strain into reserved glass. Garnish with shrimp, celery, and lemon.

The Bloody Southern

The Bloody Mary is a necessity of Sunday brunches in the South, and so to accommodate the local thirst for this scrumptious, red concoction, mixologists at the Southern Kitchen & Bar in Birmingham, Alabama, tweak the traditional pick-me-up into an adventure and an art. Nothing says "Good morning!" in Birmingham like the Bloody Southern.

2 tablespoons Smoked Sea Salt
Lime wedge
1½ ounces Chipotle Pepper-Infused Vodka*
Splash of Dark Beer (stout or porter)
Zing Zang Bloody Mary Mix
Sweet Pepper stuffed with aged Provolone Cheese and Prosciutto, for garnish

Spread smoked sea salt on a small plate. Rub the rim of a pint glass with the lime wedge, and dip rim in the salt. Add cracked ice to the glass; set aside. Combine vodka, beer, and Bloody Mary mix in a mixing glass with cracked ice. Stir to combine, and strain into prepared glass. Garnish with stuffed pepper.

*Chipotle Pepper–Infused Vodka: Pour contents of a 750 ml bottle of vodka into a pitcher with a lid. Wrap contents of 1 (4-ounce) can of chipotle peppers in a clean cotton cloth to dry; add to vodka. Allow to sit until vodka changes color, at least 2 hours.

Mi Michelada

Along with traditional Mexican street fare, Brooklyn's Gran Electrica serves this tart, slightly sweet and salty Michelada (pronounced *mee-che-LAH-dah*), a kind of a Bloody Mary made with beer instead of vodka, created for the restaurant by Tamer Hamawi—with a respectful nod to South of the Border.

1 tablespoon Celery Salt
1 tablespoon Chile Piquin
6 dashes Valentina Hot Sauce
4 dashes Worcestershire
2 ounces Clamato Juice, chilled
1 ounce Lime Juice, freshly squeezed
12-ounce can Tecate Beer
Cucumber stick (cut taller than the pint glass), for garnish

Spread the mix of celery salt and chile piquin on a small plate. Rub the rim of a tall glass with the lime wedge and dip rim in the spice mix. Coat the inside of a pint glass with hot sauce, then build over ice all remaining ingredients. Top up with the beer, reserving remainder to top up as you drink. Garnish with cucumber.

Bloody Masterpiece

It's a Bloody Mary "with the works" at Sobelman's Pub & Grill, the Milwaukee, Wisconsin, institution, where Dave Sobelman believes the epic drink should also function as a full breakfast. Ostentatious and fully loaded, his version contains a dozen different garnishes, including a cheeseburger slider (all served with a chaser of local Sprecher Beer on the side). It's a "morning-after" breakfast not for the faint of heart.

2 ounces Vodka
Jimmy Luv's Bloody Mary Mix
1 Celery stalk
1 Pickled Polish Sausage
1 cube Colby Jack Cheese
1 large boiled and chilled Shrimp
1 Grape Tomato
1 Lemon wedge
1 Pickled Brussels Sprout
1 Pickled Mushroom
1 Pickled Onion
1 Pickled Asparagus
1 Green Onion
1 Cheeseburger Slider on a stick

Combine vodka and Bloody Mary mix in a 16-ounce mason jar filled with ice. Dress with assorted garnishes.

CHAMPAGNE COCKTAIL

The Champagne Cocktail, sometimes called "Chorus Girl's Milk," is one of the oldest of cocktails. Dating as far back as 1862, it was referenced in "Professor" Jerry Thomas's *Bartenders Guide: How To Mix Drinks*; although, Thomas, "the father of American mixology," calls for shaking the ingredients, including the sparkling wine, which is surely a *faux pas*. Etiquette authority Amy Vanderbilt once explained that Champagne Cocktails, sweetened up with lumps of sugar and slightly discolored with bitters, came about as an attempt "to enhance an inferior Champagne." In cinema, Victor Laszlo and Captain Renault both order Champagne Cocktails in the 1942 classic *Casablanca*, and Deborah Kerr and Cary Grant sipped cocktails made with pink Champagne in *An Affair to Remember*.

Ritz Champagne Cocktail

Ah, the Ritz Bar, that society rendezvous just inside the discreet Rue Cambon entrance to the legendary hotel, appointed with red velvet armchairs and Victorian furnishings, a marble fireplace and historic portraits. This is where the Champagne Cocktail hit its stride in the 1920s, attracting such notables as Ernest Hemingway, F. Scott Fitzgerald, and Cole Porter. Journalist Basil Woon reported that, every morning at half-past seven, Porter would leap out of bed and arrange himself in a riding habit. Then, after writing a song or two, he would appear at the stroke of half-past twelve at the Ritz Bar, where he would say, "Champagne Cocktail, please. Had a marvelous ride this morning!"

1 sugar cube
3 dashes Angostura Bitters
Champagne, chilled
Lemon peel, for garnish

Place sugar cube in Champagne coupe glass; soak with bitters. Top up with Champagne. Express lemon peel over the glass, rub it around the rim, and drop it in.

Savoy Champagne Cocktail

The American Bar at the Savoy Hotel was one of the earliest establishments to introduce American-style cocktails to Europe. Luckily for the Savoy faithful, the arrival of Prohibition forced barman Harry Craddock to flee New York's Knickerbocker Bar for the more permissive shores of England, although not before reputedly shaking the last legal cocktail to be served in the city. Once ensconced behind mahogany at the Savoy Bar, he added richness and gravitas to a glass of Champagne.

1 Sugar Cube
3 dashes Angostura Bitters
½ ounce Cognac
½ ounce Grand Marnier
Champagne, chilled
Orange peel, for garnish

Place sugar cube in Champagne coupe glass; soak with bitters. Add cognac and Grand Marnier. Top up with Champagne. Express orange peel over the glass, rub it around the rim, and drop it in.

Buck's Fizz

Captain H. J. Buckmaster of the Royal Horse Guards established the Buck's Club, a venerable gentlemen's club in London in 1919 (whose membership included Winston Churchill). The Buck's Fizz was concocted in 1921 by barman Malachy "Pat" MacGarry at the club's American Cocktail Bar, a less stuffy and more convivial gathering place than had previously existed in British gentlemen's clubs.

Orange Juice, chilled
Champagne, chilled

Fill a chilled Champagne flute ⅔ full of orange juice. Top up with Champagne.

French 75

Alec Waugh, author of *In Praise of Wine & Certain Noble Spirits*, calls the French 75 "the most powerful drink in the world." The name came from 75 mm howitzers placed along the Maginot Line during World War I, and much like the weapon, according to barman Harry Craddock of the London Savoy, the cocktail "hits with remarkable precision." Society journalist Lucius Beebe, who it is said could "drink a double bottle of Champagne without batting an eye," authored *The Stork Club Bar Book* in 1946, providing the club's recipe for "the celebrated French 75." (Substitute bourbon for the gin to make the French 95, and cognac in place of gin for a French 125.)

2 ounces Gin
Juice of ½ Lemon
1 teaspoon Powdered Sugar
Champagne, chilled

Combine gin, lemon juice, and sugar to a mixing glass filled with cracked ice. Shake vigorously, and strain into a Champagne coupe glass. Top up with Champagne.

Jimmie Roosevelt

In 1939, *Town and Country* magazine sent Charles H. Baker, Jr. on assignment around the world to find the very best food and drink. The result was *The Gentleman's Companion*, a grand cocktail tour that takes the reader on imaginative flights fueled by drinks like the Champagne Cocktail he christened after the oldest son of President Franklin D. Roosevelt. "It is cooling, refreshing, invigorating, a delight to the eye and palate," writes Baker.

1 lump Sugar
5 dashes Angostura Bitters
2 ounces Cognac
Champagne, chilled
2 tablespoons Green Chartreuse

Fill a big 16-ounce thin crystal goblet with finely cracked ice. Saturate the sugar with bitters and place in the center. Add cognac, and top up with Champagne. Carefully float chartreuse over the top.

She Couldn't Say No

"Champagne is the ebullient ambassador with plenary powers at the Court of Ebriety," writes Crosby Gaige in his 1941 *Cocktail Guide and Ladies' Companion*. He provides this rendering of the Champagne Cocktail as a "toast to the bride."

Juice of 1 Lemon
1 ounce Gin
1 teaspoon Sugar
5 dashes Angostura Bitters
Champagne, chilled

Combine ingredients in a mixing glass with cracked ice. Shake vigorously, and strain into an 8-ounce highball glass with new ice. Top up with Champagne.

Mimosa

Roots of the Mimosa, which sprouted a few short years after the Buck's Fizz, blossomed in the Ritz Bar in Paris, where barman Frank Meier went heavier on the Champagne and named the sparkling union after its similarity in color to a flower called mimosa, favored by French gardeners. Meier later created an alternate version to the Mimosa, adding a splash of apricot brandy and calling it a Valencia.

Orange Juice, chilled
Champagne, chilled

Fill a chilled Champagne flute ⅓ full of orange juice. Top up with Champagne.

Bellini

Opened by bartender Giuseppe Cipriani at Calle Vallaresso in Venice, Italy, in 1931, Harry's Bar has long been frequented by famous people, including Ernest Hemingway, Truman Capote, Maria Callas, Orson Welles, and Aristotle Onassis. The Bellini, invented by Mr. Cipriani sometime between 1934 and 1948 and named after fifteenth-century Venetian painter Giovanni Bellini, is revered as an Italian lifeline to civilization. The refreshing, low-alcohol Bellini contains no spirits, yet it's still considered a cocktail.

Peach Purée
Prosecco, or other sparkling wine, chilled

Pour peach purée into chilled Champagne flute, and gently add Prosecco. Stir gently. Proper proportions call for ⅓ peach purée and ⅔ chilled sparkling wine (make sure to pour the purée into the glass first).

Death in the Afternoon

Ernest Hemingway is credited with creating this drink at Harry's New York Bar in Paris sometime during the 1930s after becoming a fan of absinthe. The cocktail shares its name with the author's book, *Death in the Afternoon*, about the ceremony and traditions of Spanish bullfighting. His recipe was first shared in *So Red the Nose, or Breath in the Afternoon*, a 1935 cocktail book with contributions from famous authors. Hemingway's advice: "Drink three to five of these slowly."

2 ounces Absinthe (or Pernod)
Champagne, chilled

Add absinthe to a chilled Champagne coupe glass. Top up with Champagne.

Champagne Cocktail Gloria Swanson

Lucius Beebe (*The Stork Club Bar Book*) writes: "Glamourous and worldly Gloria Swanson, a celebrity unabashed in her tastes and determined on the best, likes to start the day with what, within the memory of the author used to have been known on the Continent as 'Kings Ruin' because it was the traditional favorite of so many of the old, bearded kings of Europe who used to frequent Foyot's, the Cafe de Paris, Maxim's, and the Ritz in the days when the going for kings was good." The Stork Club served Miss Swanson's eponymous cocktail in a tall Tom Collins glass.

2 ounces Cognac
Champagne, chilled
Lemon peel, for garnish

Add cognac to a tall glass half-filled with ice. Top up with Champagne. Express lemon peel over the glass, rub it around the rim, and drop it in.

Chicago Cocktail

Chicago Sun-Times columnist Irv Kupcinet called Chez Paree "the most glamorous night club in history." Located on the city's Magnificent Mile, Chez Paree became Chicago's most famous watering hole as it emerged from the bootlegging and speakeasy scene of the 1920s. Patrons sipped the club's own Champagne Cocktail while being entertained by headliners such as Nat King Cole, Louis Armstrong, Frank Sinatra, Tony Bennett, Bob Hope, Milton Berle, Carol Channing, Joey Bishop, Buddy Hackett, Sophie Tucker, Jimmy Durante, Martin & Lewis, and Joe E. Lewis.

1½ ounces Brandy
¾ ounce Triple Sec
1 dash Angostura Bitters
Champagne, chilled

Combine brandy, triple sec, and bitters in a mixing glass with cracked ice. Shake vigorously, and strain into a chilled Champagne coupe glass. Top up with Champagne.

Hell and High Water

Ted Shane's *Bar Guide* was published by *True Magazine* in 1950, "dedicated to folks who value their lives, friends, futures, homes, and taste buds, and like to shake up a few for conviviality's sake." The drink may have been inspired by George Lippard's nineteenth-century novel *Empire City*, in which a character is described as "wrapped up in an atmosphere of brandy and Champagne—on fire with the flames of alcohol—the very sublimest type of Satan in liquor."

2 ounces Brandy
1 teaspoon Lemon Juice, freshly squeezed
1 teaspoon Grenadine
Champagne, chilled

Combine brandy, lemon juice, and grenadine in a mixing glass with cracked ice. Shake vigorously, and strain into a chilled Champagne coupe glass. Top up with Champagne.

Velvet Swing

Flamboyant nineteenth-century architect Stanford White maintained a private lair on Twenty-Fourth Street in Manhattan where he entertained scantily clad chorus girls on a red velvet swing, hung from the ceiling with ivy-twined ropes. The story was told in *The Girl in the Red Velvet Swing*, a 1955 film starring Joan Collins, followed by the introduction of a red-hued Champagne Cocktail. Bartender Mikey Morrow's version is served at Toronto's Table 17.

Granulated Sugar, for rim
Lemon wedge
½ ounce Taylor Fladgate LBV Port

¼ ounce Hennessey V.S Cognac
Cava (or other sparkling wine), chilled
Lemon peel, for garnish

Spread sugar on a small plate. Rub the rim of a Champagne flute with the lemon wedge, and dip rim in the sugar. Set aside. Add port to a mixing glass with cracked ice, and stir to chill. Strain into the prepared flute, and top up with sparkling wine. Use the back of a teaspoon to gently float cognac on top. Express lemon peel over the glass, wrap around a cocktail pick, and place at the edge of the flute.

The Dame

In *The Big Sleep*, as Philip Marlowe gets drawn into the affairs of the Sternwoods, the aged patriarch tells the shamus, "I used to like my brandy with Champagne—the Champagne as cold as Valley Forge and about a third of a glass of brandy beneath it." The suggestion is well taken by barkeeps Jared Meisler and Damian Windsor at The Roger Room in West Hollywood, California, with a brandy-spiked sipper, sweetened and colorized with ruby-red cherry liqueur.

1 ounce Courvoisier VSOP
½ ounce Cherry Heering
¼ ounce Lemon Juice, freshly squeezed

Sparkling Rosé, chilled
Maraschino Cherry, for garnish

Combine cognac, Cherry Heering, and lemon juice in a mixing glass with cracked ice. Shake vigorously, and strain into a chilled Champagne flute. Top up with sparkling rosé, and drop cherry into the glass.

Brooklyn Bee

Under the relentless guidance of Eric Ripert, Le Bernardin serves classically rooted seafood cuisine at its most resplendent. This lavender- and honey-kissed cocktail with a splash of sparkling Cava—the Spanish answer to Champagne—pairs effortlessly with Mr. Ripert's signature cooking.

1¾ ounces Brooklyn Gin
1 ounce Lavender Honey Syrup*
½ ounce Lemon Juice, freshly squeezed
Absinthe, for rinse
Cava (Brut), chilled
Lavender Tea, for mist
Lavender sprig, for garnish

Rinse a chilled Champagne coupe glass with absinthe and set aside. Combine the remaining ingredients (except the sparkling wine) in a cocktail shaker with ice and shake. Strain into the prepared glass, top up with sparkling wine, and mist with a spritz of lavender tea. Garnish with lavender sprig.

*Lavender Honey Syrup: Steep ¼ cup of dried lavender in 1½ cups of near-boiling water for 15 minutes. Strain, measure the liquid, and stir in an equal amount of honey. Let cool to room temperature, refrigerate, and use within 2 weeks.

Dead Man Walking

The bar program at Levant, Scott Snyder's Arabesque restaurant in Portland, Oregon, is run by Abel Beazley, who revamps a French 75–inspired cocktail into a cultivated after-dinner refreshment, sweetened with liqueur made from Marasca cherries and deepened with bittersweet aromas of Italian digestivo.

¼ ounce Campari, for rinse
¾ ounce Tanqueray Gin
½ ounce Lemon Juice, freshly squeezed

½ ounce Luxardo Maraschino liqueur
½ ounce Barolo Chinato
Prosecco, chilled

Rinse a cocktail coupe glass with Campari, and discard the excess. Combine the remaining ingredients (except the Prosecco) in a cocktail shaker with ice, and shake. Strain into the prepared coupe, and top up with Prosecco.

He Whispered in Her Ear

Wood is a low-lit, low-key Chicago hangout where drinksmith Tommy J. Lansaw prepares a dry, herbaceous hybrid of a Martini and a Champagne Cocktail—glamorized with the bubbles and bouquet of Cava, the sparkling wine produced in Spain's Catalonia region.

¼ ounce Chareau Aloe Vera Liqueur, for rinse
2 ounces Caorunn Scottish Gin
½ ounce Imbue "Petal & Thorn" Bittersweet
   Vermouth

2 drops Organic Thyme Oil
Cava Brut (or other dry sparkling wine), chilled
Sprig of fresh Thyme, for garnish

Rinse a cocktail coupe glass with aloe vera liqueur, and discard the excess. In a mixing glass with cracked ice, combine gin, vermouth, and thyme oil. Stir briskly, and strain into the prepared glass. Top up with cava, and garnish with thyme sprig.

Pure Poison

Bartender asks a patron, *"What's your poison?"* The answer at London's Salt Whisky Bar & Dining Room is a nimble, fruit-forward cocktail with rich textures and festive bubbles that play with a broad range of flavors. The hint of mint adds an aromatic nose to complement the sweet-tart potion.

1 ounce Vodka
⅔ ounce Midori
⅓ ounce Orgeat Syrup
⅓ ounce Lime Juice, freshly squeezed

¼ slice of an apple
Champagne, chilled
Mint sprig, for garnish

Muddle apple in a mixing glass, then add all ingredients (except Champagne) with cracked ice. Shake vigorously, and strain into a red wine glass filled with crushed ice. Top up with Champagne, and garnish with mint.

The Mistress

It's an industrial cathedral, crafted from the architectural artifacts of the first power plant in downtown Los Angeles. The Edison's signature libation pays homage to the ascendency of the Champagne Cocktail in the 1920s with an adventurous variation, electrified with vodka, and amplified with luscious lemon and pomegranate. Prosecco provides the spark.

1 ounce Vodka
½ ounce Limoncello
1 ounce Pomegranate Juice
Prosecco, chilled
1 fresh Blackberry, for garnish

Combine vodka, limoncello, and pomegranate juice in a mixing glass. Shake vigorously, and strain into a chilled Champagne coupe glass. Top up with Prosecco, and drop a blackberry into the glass.

Nguyen Dynasty

Named for the last ruling family of Vietnam, who defeated the Tay Son Dynasty, Jon Christiansen of Seattle's Ba Bar transforms the vintage Gin Fizz into a Champagne Cocktail designed to work in tandem with Chef Eric Banh's distinctive take on Vietnamese-inspired food.

1 ounce Gin
¾ ounce Rhubarb Syrup*
½ ounce Lemon Juice, freshly squeezed
Prosecco, chilled
Star Anise, for garnish

Combine gin, rhubarb syrup, and lemon juice in a mixing glass with cracked ice. Shake vigorously, and double-strain into a chilled Champagne coupe glass. Top up with Prosecco, and drop star anise into the glass.

*Rhubarb Syrup:
16 ounces Rhubarb, diced
16 ounces Sugar
Peels of Lime and Orange
16 ounces Water
1 ounce Lemon Juice
½ ounce Vodka

In a small pot, combine rhubarb, sugar, and peels of lime and orange with water, and bring to a boil. Reduce the heat to moderately low, and simmer until slightly thickened and bright pink in color, about 20 minutes. Let the syrup cool; then pour through a fine-mesh sieve set over a bowl. Press down gently, and discard the solids. Add lemon juice and vodka to preserve. Store in fridge until ready to use.

Million Dollar Dream

During the mid-1800s, British Army soldiers mixed black tea and rum in a drink they called "Gunfire." During the same period, Americans fortified tea with rum into Hot Toddies as a prescription for chilly winter nights. At Rye on Market in Louisville, Kentucky, Bradley Hammond employs the historic fusion of tea and rum in an effervescent cocktail with a refreshing citrus finish.

1 ounce Plantation 3 Star Light Rum
½ ounce Lime Juice, freshly squeezed
½ ounce Earl Grey Honey Syrup*
2 dashes Bittermens Tiki Bitters
Cremant de Limoux (or other sparkling wine), chilled
Lime peel, for garnish

Combine rum, lime juice, honey syrup, and bitters in a mixing glass. Shake vigorously, and strain into a chilled Champagne coupe glass. Top up with Prosecco. Express lime peel over the glass, rub it around the rim, and drop it in.

*Earl Grey Honey Syrup:
1 teaspoon loose leaf Earl Grey Tea (or 1 tea bag)
1 cup warm Water
3 ounces Honey

Soak Earl Grey tea in 1 cup warm water for 1 hour. Pour the tea into a saucepan, and bring to a boil. Leave the bag/loose tea in the pan. Add honey, and simmer for 10 minutes. Remove from heat, and double-strain into a clean (sterile) bottle.

Perfect Thyming

Commander's Palace, nestled in the heart of the tree-lined Garden District, is a New Orleans land-mark that dates back to 1880. Born and raised in the Big Easy, bar chef Ferrel Dugas dresses her Champagne Cocktail to the nines with Bourbon, a splash of praline liqueur, and lemony aromatics of fresh thyme.

1½ ounces Benchmark Bourbon
½ ounce Praline Liqueur
½ ounce Lemon Juice, freshly squeezed
½ ounce Simple Syrup

1 sprig + 1 additional, for garnish, fresh Lemon Thyme
Champagne, chilled

Muddle 1 sprig of thyme in a mixing glass. Add the first four ingredients with ice. Shake vigorously, and double strain into a chilled Champagne coupe glass. Top up with Champagne. Garnish with second spring of thyme.

~~~~~~

Midnight in Paris

It's a Toronto bistro that resembles a 1920s Parisian cocktail lounge. Michael Mooney is bar manager at Geraldine, where the bubbles rise in style. He pays homage to the bygone era with a Chartreuse-instilled, absinthe-soaked libation, refreshed with cucumber, and animated with sparkling wine from the Jura region of France.

3 slices Cucumber + 1 additional for garnish
1 ounce Lucid Absinthe
½ ounce Yellow Chartreuse
¾ ounce Lime Juice, freshly squeezed

½ ounce Simple Syrup
Crémant du Jura Brut (or other dry sparkling wine), chilled

Muddle 3 slices of cucumber in the bottom of a mixing glass. Add absinthe, Chartreuse, lime, simple syrup, and fill with ice. Shake vigorously, and double-strain into a chilled Champagne coupe glass. Top up with the sparkling wine, and garnish with cucumber slice.

La Vie en Rose

At the Toronto Temperance Society, Oliver Stern takes inspiration from French cabaret singer Édith Piaf's ode to lifelong love, translated as "Life in Rosy Hues" or "Life through Rose-Colored Glasses." Rosé sparkling wine adds a lovely twist and pink hue to a subtly shaped Canadian version of the classic cocktail.

1½ ounces Absolute Elyx
1½ ounces Lemon Grapefruit Cordial*

Dry Sparkling Rosé, chilled
Grapefruit peel, for garnish

Combine ingredients (except sparkling rosé) in a mixing glass with cracked ice. Shake vigorously, and strain into a chilled Champagne coupe glass. Top up with sparkling rosé. Express grapefruit peel over the glass, rub it around the rim, and drop it in.

*Lemon Grapefruit Cordial:
Zest of 5 Lemons
Zest of 2 large Grapefruits
1 cup Lemon Juice
1 cup Grapefruit Juice
1½ cups Sugar
1½ ounces over-proof Vodka

In a container, place zests of lemons and grapefruits (micro plane is the best tool for this). Add lemon juice, grapefruit juice, and sugar (add over-proof vodka to increase shelf life). Refrigerate for 24 hours, then strain through cheesecloth.

Three Naked Ladies

Morgan Nevans of Café Luxembourg brings a dash of glamour to New York's Upper West Side with a bubbly concoction named for the famous photo of three nudes standing at bar with their backs—and bare bottoms—to the camera. "We consider absinthe, St. Germain, and Champagne the 'ladies' of the cocktail," explains Mr. Nevans, "and always use true Champagne, not sparkling wine."

¼ ounce Absinthe
½ ounce St. Germain
¼ ounce Lemon Juice, freshly squeezed
Heidsieck Monopole Blue Top (or other Champagne), chilled
Lemon peel, for garnish

Combine ingredients (except Champagne) in a mixing glass with cracked ice. Shake vigorously, and strain into a chilled Champagne flute. Top up with Champagne. Express lemon peel over the glass, rub it around the rim, and drop it in.

Beauty School Dropout

It's a drink that is at once bright, citrusy, and faintly floral. Constructed by Krista Kemple at Decca Restaurant in Louisville, Kentucky, the sparkling sipper borrows from multiple prototypes in Champagne Cocktail history—spiked with an assertive juniper spirit, tinged with aromatic bitters, and dolled up with grapefruit essence.

1½ ounces Junípero Gin
6 dashes of Peychaud's Bitters
1 ounce Lemon Juice, freshly squeezed

1 ounce Simple Syrup
Champagne, chilled
Grapefruit peel, for garnish

Combine ingredients (except Champagne) in a mixing glass with cracked ice. Shake vigorously, and strain into a chilled Champagne coupe glass. Top up with Champagne. Express grapefruit peel over the glass, rub it around the rim, and drop it in.

Thai 75

The French 75 takes its name from an artillery weapon favored by French troops due to its wicked fire power, a not-so-subtle nod to the drink's lethalness. In Miami Beach, patrons of the Khong River House are "transported" to an Asian street emporium with flavors and traditions of the Northern Thailand region. Khong's version of the classic cocktail softens the bite of gin with lychee purée and binds ingredients with lemongrass syrup to create a fuller, more harmonious mouthfeel.

1 ounce Nolet's Gin
½ ounce Lychee Purée
½ ounce Lemongrass Simple Syrup*

Champagne, chilled
Lychee nut, speared, for garnish

Combine gin, lychee purée, and simple syrup in a mixing glass with cracked ice. Shake vigorously, and strain into a chilled Champagne flute. Top up with Champagne, and garnish with speared lychee nut.

*Lemongrass Simple Syrup: Place 2 lemongrass stalks, 2 cups of water, and 1 cup of sugar in a saucepan, and bring to a boil. Reduce heat, and simmer, partially covered, for 15 minutes. Strain the mixture, and cool.

Femme Fatale

Bette Davis once said, "There comes a time in every woman's life when the only thing that helps is a glass of Champagne." Ms. Davis would surely approve of the vigilant mixologists at NoMa Social in New Rochelle, New York, who embrace Champagne's flirtation with strawberries and sweet/tart lemon. Invite the girls over for brunch.

2 or 3 fresh Strawberries + 1 additional for garnish
1 teaspoon Sugar
1 ounce Limoncello
Champagne, chilled

Muddle fresh strawberries with sugar in a mixing glass. Fill with ice, and add limoncello. Shake vigorously, and strain into a chilled Martini glass. Top up with Champagne, and garnish with strawberry.

Catherine Deneuve

Once pronounced the world's most beautiful woman, French cinema goddess Catherine Deneuve inspires a sparkling cocktail, created by mixologist Marcin Bilski at the Cellar Door, a quirky underground cocktail bar in Covent Garden, London. The clever pairing of gin with fresh cucumber is first scented with elderflowers and citrus, then animated with Champagne froth.

1 ounce Hendricks Gin
½ ounce fresh Cucumber Juice
1 dash Lemon Juice, freshly squeezed
1 dash Elderflower Cordial

1 dash Simple Syrup
Champagne, chilled
Cucumber slice, for garnish

Combine ingredients (except Champagne) in a mixing glass with cracked ice. Shake vigorously, and strain into a chilled Champagne flute. Top up with Champagne. Garnish with cucumber.

Lady Germain

Chris Hannah is one of New Orleans's most beloved bartenders, manning the historic French 75 Bar attached to Arnaud's Restaurant, where he turns out impeccable cocktails with a reverence for the history that accompanies them. Mr. Hannah honors eighteenth century Lady Germain, a wealthy French aristocrat and courtier, with a Champagne potion seasoned with strawberry and perfumed with elderflower blossoms.

1 ripe Strawberry
1¼ ounces London Dry Gin
¼ ounce Lemon Juice, freshly squeezed

½ ounce St. Germain
Champagne, chilled
Lemon peel, for garnish

Muddle the strawberry in a mixing glass, add the next three ingredients, and shake with ice. Double-strain into a chilled Champagne flute, and top up with Champagne. Express lemon peel over the glass, rub it around the rim, and drop it in.

DAIQUIRI

It was 1898, the year America helped Cuba defeat Spain in their War of Independence. After supervising work at the iron mines in Daiquiri, Cuba, American mining engineers gathered at the Venus Bar in nearby Santiago for liquid refreshment, sipping local rum over cracked ice with sugar and freshly squeezed limes. History holds that Jennings Cox, general manager of the Spanish American Iron Company, was responsible for naming the drink after the Cuban village. In 1902, William Astor "Willie" Chanler, intent on investing in iron ore, visited the region where he was introduced to the drink. It was the well-connected Chanler, member of the Knickerbocker Club, Union Club, Players Club, Lambs Club, New York Yacht Club, Meadowbrook Polo Club, and Metropolitan Club, who helped popularize the daiquiri cocktail in New York.

Daiquiri No. 1

After José Abeal emigrated from Spain to Cuba in 1904, he found work as a bartender in Havana. With the help of Valentin Garcia, owner of La Gran Via bakery, Abeal purchased what was then a small grocery store and turned it into Sloppy Joe's Bar. His staff of *cantineros* was guided by Fabio Delgado Fuentes, "the Father of All Cocktail Makers." Among the world's greats who dropped in for a sip were the Duke of Windsor, Jean-Paul Sartre, Errol Flynn, Gary Cooper, Clark Gable, Spencer Tracey, and Greta Garbo. The formula for Daiquiri No. 1 was recorded in *Sloppy Joe's Cocktails Manual* (1931).

2 or 3 ounces Bacardi Rum
1 teaspoon Powdered Sugar
Juice of 1 or 2 Limes

Into a tall glass packed with cracked ice, add sugar, squeeze limes, then pour rum. Stir with a long-handled spoon until the glass is frosted.

El Floridita Daiquiri

El Floridita, the legendary bar at the corner of Obispo and Monserrate Streets in the heart of Old Havana was the "laboratory" of *cantinero* Constante Ribalaigua, where he experimented with ingredients and tinkered with the original daiquiri recipe. Sometime in the 1930s, he added maraschino and cracked ice, then blended everything together in an electric blender to create a "frappé" texture for the first frozen daiquiri.

2 ounces Bacardi Rum
½ teaspoon superfine Sugar
1 teaspoon Maraschino Liqueur
½ ounce Lime Juice
2 cups finely cracked Ice

Combine ingredients in a blender. Blend until smooth, and pour into cocktail coupe glass.

Mary Pickford

During Prohibition, Havana was Mecca for thirsty Americans, and the luxurious Gran Hotel Sevilla (later called the Sevilla Biltmore), whose elegant, air-conditioned bar was decorated by famous Cuban caricaturist Conrado Massager, became the social center of the city. During his stint at the Sevilla, barman Eddie Woelke created this daiquiri variant in honor of "America's Sweetheart," silent screen actress Mary Pickford.

2 ounces Rum
2 ounces unsweetened Pineapple Juice
½ teaspoon Grenadine Syrup

Combine ingredients in a mixing glass with cracked ice. Shake vigorously, and strain into a chilled cocktail coupe glass.

El Presidente

In 1928, British playwright and journalist Basil Woon published a colorful portrait of Prohibition-era Havana entitled *When It's Cocktail Time in Cuba*. In his book, Woon detailed his encounters in the country's casinos, country clubs, and, of course, its cocktail bars. He cited the daiquiri as the most popular refreshment of the "earnest drinkers of Havana," and cited the El Presidente, named in honor of President Gerardo Machado (who promised to make Cuba the "Switzerland of the Americas"), as "the aristocrat of cocktails and the one preferred by the better class of Cubans."

1½ ounces Rum
1½ ounces Dry Vermouth
1 teaspoon Orange Curaçao
1 dash Grenadine Syrup
Orange peel, for garnish

Combine ingredients in a mixing glass with cracked ice. Shake vigorously, and strain into cocktail coupe glass. Express orange peel over the glass, rub it around the rim, and drop it in.

Ace of Clubs

The Ace of Clubs Lounge on Front Street and the corner of Parliament in Hamilton, Bermuda, attracted American tourists during the 1930s. The house cocktail was a twist on the daiquiri, preserved in the pages of *Esquire* magazine. The crème de cacao gives it an intriguing depth of flavor without dominating the mix.

2 ounces Rum
½ ounce White Crème de Cacao
½ ounce Lime Juice
½ teaspoon Simple Syrup

Combine ingredients in a mixing glass with cracked ice. Shake vigorously, and strain into cocktail coupe glass.

Hemingway Daiquiri

Ernest Hemmingway once said, "I drink to make other people more interesting," and during his time in Cuba, he did his drinking at El Floridita. As early as 1939, Charles Baker was referring to the "new style" of blender daiquiri, like the sugarless version prepared for "Papa" Hemingway by *cantinero* Constante Ribalaigua, one that gives an already exceptional drink a bit of depth and gravity. "Remember please," wrote Baker, "that a too-sweet daiquiri is like a lovely lady with too much perfume."

2½ ounces Bacardi Rum
1 ounce Rose's Lime Juice
1 ounce Grapefruit Juice
1 splash Grenadine Syrup

Combine rum, lime juice, and grapefruit juice in a mixing glass with cracked ice. Shake vigorously, and strain into cocktail coupe glass. Add splash of grenadine over the top.

Bacardi Cocktail

The daiquiri was born using Bacardi rum, the smooth, light-bodied spirit, first produced by Don Facundo Bacardí Massó in Santiago de Cuba in 1862. American tourists flocked to the island as Prohibition shuttered bars and made alcoholic beverages illegal across the US. "Fly with us to Havana, and you can bathe in Bacardi rum two hours from now," suggested an ad by Pan American Airways, promoting its flights linking Miami with Cuba. This cousin of the daiquiri, with a dash of grenadine, was named for the brand by barman Eddie Woelke.

2 ounces Bacardi Rum
1 ounce Lemon or Lime Juice
½ ounce Grenadine Syrup
1 Lime wedge, for garnish

Combine ingredients in a mixing glass with cracked ice. Shake vigorously, and strain into cocktail coupe glass. Garnish with lime.

Mulata

According to *El Sexto Sentido del Barman* (*The Barman's Sixth Sense*) by Héctor Zumbado Argueta, the Mulata daiquiri was created in the 1940s by Cuban barman Jose Maria Vazquez, named for the contrast of ingredients (the term for black and white ancestry is used in Latin America and the Caribbean without negative connotations).

2 ounces Light Rum
1 ounce Dark Crème de Cacao
1 ounce Lime Juice
1 teaspoon Brown Sugar
Lime wedge, for garnish

Combine ingredients in a mixing glass with cracked ice. Shake vigorously, and strain into cocktail coupe glass. Garnish with lime.

Mojito

Its roots date to the "El Draque," made with sugarcane-based Tafia (a crude forerunner of rum), sugar, lime, and mint—a drink responsible for saving Sir Francis Drake's scurvy-stricken sailors in the Caribbean. In 1942, Angel Martinez opened a small, often raucous bar on Havana's Empedrado Street that became known as La Bodeguita del Medio and where the mojito first came to fame. Gabriel García Márquez, Errol Flynn, and Marlene Dietrich were all regulars at La Bodeguita, and Ernest Hemingway once scrawled "My mojito in La Bodeguita, my daiquiri in El Floridita" across the backbar.

6 Mint leaves (plus 1 sprig for garnish)
2 teaspoons Sugar
¾ ounce Lime Juice

2 ounces Bacardi Rum
Soda Water

Muddle 6 mint leaves, sugar, and lime juice in a tall glass. Add rum. Fill glass with ice, and top up with soda. Garnish with mint sprig.

Q. B. Cooler

The "Q.B." stands for "Quiet Birdmen," a drinking club for aviators which included Charles Lindbergh among its members. Donn Beach (Don the Beachcomber), adventurer, restaurateur, and "Founding Father of Tiki Bars," created this homage, among other potent rum cocktails, in 1934 for his first café in Hollywood, California. (The Q.B. Cooler is said to be the inspiration for "Trader Vic" Bergeron's Mai Tai, first served in his Oakland, California restaurant in 1944).

2 ounces Dark Rum
1 ounce Light Rum
½ ounce Lime Juice
½ ounce Orange Juice

¼ ounce Passion Fruit Syrup
⅛ teaspoon Pernod
Dash Angostura Bitters
Mint sprig, for garnish

Combine ingredients in a blender with 12 ounces of crushed ice. Blend for 6 seconds, then transfer to a tall glass. Add additional ice to fill, and then garnish the cocktail with the mint sprig; serve immediately.

Margarita

It's a daiquiri, exchanging rum for tequila, orangey triple sec instead of sugar, and salting the rim of the glass (to ease the "bite"). There are many legends about who invented the Margarita Cocktail. Many believe that Margaret "Margarita" Sames, a wealthy Dallas socialite, created the drink in her Acapulco holiday home in 1948. Others claim that a bartender in Tijuana created it to impress actress Rita Hayworth, whose birth name was Margarita.

2 tablespoons Kosher Salt, for garnish
1½ ounces Tequila
½ ounce Triple Sec

1 ounce Lime Juice
1 Lime wedge, for garnish

Spread salt on a small plate. Rub the rim of a tall glass with the lime wedge, and dip rim in the salt. Add ice to the glass; set aside. Combine tequila, triple sec, and lime juice in a mixing glass with cracked ice. Shake vigorously, and strain into prepared glass. Garnish with lime.

Hurricane

During Prohibition, the speakeasy was known as Mr. O'Brien's Club Tipperary, and a password ("storm's brewin'") was required to gain entrance. In the mid-1940s, partners Pat O'Brien and Charley Cantrell created a new drink to help them move some of the rum that local distributors forced them to buy before they could get the next shipment of more popular spirits. They served the concoction in hurricane lamp-shaped glasses, and the Hurricane Cocktail became one of the most popular drinks in New Orleans' French Quarter, especially among tourists.

2 ounces Light Rum
2 ounces Dark Rum
2 ounces Passion Fruit Juice
1 ounce Orange Juice

½ ounce Lime Juice
1 tablespoon Simple Syrup
1 tablespoon Grenadine Syrup
Orange slice and Cherry, for garnish

Combine ingredients in a mixing glass with cracked ice. Shake vigorously, and strain into a Hurricane glass filled with cracked ice. Garnish with orange and cherry.

While Rome Burns

The number one bestseller for nonfiction in 1934, *While Rome Burns* includes essays on a variety of topics by Alexander Woollcott, a leading member of the Algonquin Round Table. According to *The Esquire Drink Book* (1957), it's also the name Woollcott attached to his favorite daiquiri-inspired tipple.

2 ounces Rum
1 ounce Lemon Juice
1 dash Maple Syrup

Combine ingredients in a mixing glass with cracked ice. Shake vigorously, and strain into cocktail coupe glass.

〰〰

Dumb Dora's Daiquiri

The name comes from 1920s slang, popularized by the vaudeville act of George Burns and Gracie Allen. Freya of Logan Brown Restaurant in Wellington, New Zealand, inspired by Floridita-style daiquiris of the same era, replaces maraschino liqueur with Pinot noir–cherry syrup. The result, according to the bar mistress is "a deeper sweetness complementing the tartness of the lime perfectly." The syrup is spooned over crushed ice to create a bramble-like marbling.

1½ ounces Stolen White Rum
⅔ ounce Lime Juice, freshly squeezed
⅓ ounce Simple Syrup

1 teaspoon Pinot Noir–Cherry Syrup*
Pinot Noir–soaked Cherry, for garnish

Combine rum, lime juice, and simple syrup in a mixing glass with a small scoop of ice. Shake vigorously for 10 seconds, then strain over crushed ice in a lowball glass. Spoon the cherry-wine syrup over the top, and garnish with cherry.

*Pinot Noir–Cherry Syrup: Bring 12 ounces frozen pitted dark sweet cherries (thawed) and 1 cup of Pinot noir (or other fruity, dry red wine) to a boil in a small saucepan. Reduce heat, and simmer, uncovered, for 20 minutes. Add 1 cup sugar. Cook and stir until sugar is dissolved. Remove from heat, and allow to cool to room temperature.

Night Court

A hidden gem tucked behind the lobby of New York's Iroquois Hotel, The Lantern's Keep offers this slightly richer interpretation of the classic daiquiri, inspired by the Honey Bee cocktail in Ted Saucier's *Bottoms Up* (1951). Angostura bitters create depth and complexity while a note of salt "brightens" the citrus.

2 ounces Gosling's Rum
1 ounce Lime Juice, freshly squeezed
¾ ounce Honey Syrup*

3 dashes Angostura Bitters
2 dashes Saline Solution **
Lime wheel, for garnish

Add ingredients to a mixing glass with cracked ice. Shake vigorously, and strain into a chilled cocktail coupe glass. Garnish with lime wheel.

*Honey Syrup: Combine 1 cup honey and ½ cup water in a small saucepan over medium heat, and stir until fully incorporated. Remove from heat, let cool to room temperature, and transfer to a clean glass jar.

**Saline Solution: Mix 1 part salt to 10 parts water (about ⅛ teaspoon table salt in 1 tablespoon of water).

Cry Baby, Cry

For his super-charged construct, Tony Contreras of Ox in Portland, Oregon employs an overproof, full-bodied rum, named for Lehman "Lemon" Hart, the first supplier of rum to the British Royal Navy. The spirit's bold flavors of rich molasses and burnt caramel match up with molasses notes in the sweetener, as cloves and cinnamon from the Becherovka tingle atop the tongue with every sip.

1 ounce Lemon Hart Demerara
    Rum (151-proof)
¾ ounce Becherovka Herbal Liqueur

¾ ounce Lime Juice, freshly squeezed
½ ounce Demerara Simple Syrup
1 dash Fee Brothers Black Walnut Bitters

Combine ingredients in a mixing glass with cracked ice. Shake vigorously, and double-strain into a chilled cocktail coupe glass.

White Star

Mixologist Jon Arroyo of Founding Farmers in Washington, DC, borrows the name of the British line of luxury ships as he introduces a small-batch British gin to a delightfully refreshing mojito-inspired daiquiri, adding bright citrus, fresh mint, and crisp cucumber to the cooler.

6 Mint Leaves + 1 additional for garnish
1 Cucumber slice + 1 additional for garnish
2 dashes Mint Bitters
½ ounce Lime Juice, freshly squeezed

1 ounce Hendrick's Gin
1 ounce Bacardi Heritage Rum
¾ ounce Mint Syrup
Lemon wheel, for garnish

Combine mint leaves, cucumber, bitters, and lime juice in a mixing glass and muddle with a wood pestle. Add gin, rum, and mint syrup with cracked ice, and shake vigorously. Strain into a cobbler tin filled with crushed ice. Garnish with mint, cucumber, and lemon wheel.

Apollo's Daiquiri

Clément "Créole Shrubb," a blend of white and aged rums infused with bitter orange peels and Creole spices, takes on the leading role in this daiquiri improvisation created by mixologist Andy Pope at Elixir Tonics and Treats in Manchester, England. Brazil's national spirit, the rumlike cachaça, adds a rich bouquet of fresh-cut sugarcane to the mix.

1½ ounces Clément "Créole Shrubb" Liqueur d'Orange
½ ounce Cachaça
¼ ounce Simple Syrup
1 ounce Lime Juice, freshly squeezed
Orange peel, for garnish

Combine ingredients in a mixing glass with cracked ice. Shake vigorously, and fine-strain into cocktail coupe glass. Express orange peel over the glass, rub it around the rim, and drop it in.

Havana Daydreaming

"It's a daiquiri on steroids," explains mixologist Tony Gurdian of the Imperial in Portland, Oregon. "The classic formula is magnified with orange juice as the acid (boosted with malic and citric acid allowing it have the same 'strength' as lime). Sweetness is supplied by the spicy syrup, as the calisaya adds another dimension with herbal notes and bitter tones."

1 ounce 7 Sirens Rum
¾ ounce Calisaya Liqueur
¾ ounce Orange Acid*

½ ounce Cuban Spice Syrup**
2 fresh Bay Leaves

Combine ingredients in a mixing glass with cracked ice. Shake vigorously, and double-strain into a chilled cocktail coupe glass. Garnish with bay leaves clipped to the rim.

*Orange Acid: Combine 1 pint fresh orange juice, ½ ounce citric acid, and ⅓ ounce malic acid in a bowl, and blend with a stick blender until dissolved.

**Cuban Spice Syrup: Crush 1 teaspoon cumin seeds and ½ teaspoon peppercorns in a mortar and pestle. Combine in a saucepan 2 cups of water, 2 bay leaves, and 4 oregano leaves. Simmer on medium heat for 5 minutes, then strain. Measure steeped solution, and combine with an equal measure of sugar, stirring until dissolved.

The Brooklynite

Philadelphia's One Tippling Place has resurrected and updated this cousin of the daiquiri, sweetened with honey instead of bar sugar, and first served at New York's Stork Club. The refreshment bears a close relationship to the Canchánchara, a nineteenth-century Cuban blend of rum, lemon, honey, and water, a forerunner of the classic.

2 ounces Appleton Estate 12-Year Rum
¾ ounce Lime Juice, freshly squeezed

¾ ounce Honey Syrup*
2 dashes Angostura Bitters

Combine ingredients in a mixing glass with cracked ice. Shake vigorously, and strain into a cocktail coupe glass.

* Honey Syrup: Combine 1 cup honey and 1 cup water in a small saucepan over medium heat, and stir until fully incorporated. Remove from heat, let cool to room temperature, and transfer to a clean glass jar.

Fernet Daiquiri

The eccentric libation, suggested by Harry Craddock's Prohibition-era I.B.F. Pick-Me-Up cocktail and adapted by mixologist Kenny Freeman at Houston's Anvil Bar and Refuge, calls for Fernet Branca, the Italian "medicinal" made with gentian, chamomile, bitter orange, myhrr, and saffron, among other things. As a "pick-me-up," this rum-less daiquiri is meant to be consumed in the morning, after an evening of overindulgence.

1½ ounces Fernet Branca
1 ounce Lime Juice, freshly squeezed

¾ ounce Turbinado Simple Syrup
Lime wheel, for garnish

Combine ingredients in a mixing glass with cracked ice. Shake vigorously, and strain over crushed ice into a Collins glass. Garnish with lime.

Embiggens the Soul

If you follow *The Simpsons*, you know it was mythical Springfield's founder, Jebediah Springfield, who once said, "A noble spirit embiggens the soul." The "noble spirit" at The Violet Hour (a modern Chicago speakeasy) is rum, exploited in an homage to the daiquiri, crafted with contrasting sour and sweet elements—and exactly thirteen shakes of the Angostura bottle for depth and spice.

2 ounces White Rum
¼ ounce Laphroaig 10-Year-Old Whisky
¾ ounce Saigon Cinnamon Syrup*
½ ounce Lime Juice, freshly squeezed

13 drops Angostura Bitters
1 Egg White
Lemon peel, to express

Add ingredients to a mixing glass. Shake without ice for 5 to 8 seconds. Open the shaker, add cracked ice, and shake again. Strain into a cocktail coupe glass. Express lemon peel over the top and discard.

*Saigon Cinnamon Syrup: Bring 1 cup of water to a boil. Add 1 cup demerara sugar, and stir constantly until completely dissolved. Add 1 Ceylon cinnamon stick, and simmer for 5 to 8 minutes. Remove from heat, and allow to cool. Strain the cinnamon stick, pour syrup into a bottle, and refrigerate.

Old Cuban

The drink starts with fundamental mojito ingredients—rum, sugar, mint, lime—but expands to become an upper-class cousin of the original (think of it as a Mojito Royale), created by bar mistress Audrey Saunders at New York's Pegu Club.

6 Mint leaves (plus 1 sprig for garnish)
¾ ounce Lime Juice
1 ounce Simple Syrup
1½ ounces Amber Rum

1 or 2 dashes Angostura Bitters
2 ounces Champagne, chilled
Lime slice, for garnish

Gently bruise the mint with lime juice in a shaker using a muddler or wooden spoon. Add simple syrup, rum, bitters, and cracked ice. Shake vigorously, and strain into a cocktail coupe glass. Float Champagne on top. With a knife, slit the lime slice halfway through, and pierce it with the mint sprig. Perch it on the rim of the glass.

Strawberry and Rose Petal Daiquiri

The recipe was brought to life at Rustic Stone in Dublin, Ireland, a joint effort between chef Dylan McGrath and his bar team of Evan Brennan and Anthony Ryan. Fresh strawberries complement the smooth, clean rum, adding natural sweetness and color, as rose petals transform a summertime daiquiri into a tasteful art display.

1½ ounces Havana Club 3-Year-Old Rum
½ ounce Strawberry Liqueur
1 ounce Strawberry Purée*
½ ounce Lime Juice, freshly squeezed

¼ ounce Rose Water
½ ounce Simple Syrup
Rose petals, for garnish

Combine ingredients in a mixing glass with cracked ice. Shake vigorously, and fine-strain into a chilled martini glass. Float 1 or 2 rose petals on the surface.

*Strawberry Purée: Halve 1 pint of strawberries. In a medium saucepan, combine strawberries with ¼ cup of sugar and 6 tablespoons of water, and bring to a boil, stirring to dissolve the sugar. Let cool, then add ¾ ounce of fresh lemon juice. Transfer to a blender, and purée until smooth. Pour the purée through a fine strainer into an airtight container, and refrigerate for up to 3 days.

Nelson's Blood

Rum acquired the nickname "Nelson's Blood" after the Battle of Trafalgar in which Admiral Horatio Viscount Nelson was mortally wounded. To preserve Nelson's body, it was placed in a barrel of rum. At Saltine Oyster Bar in Jackson, Mississippi, Robert Arender and Jesse Houston elevate the classic daiquiri formula with tea, spices, and a sprig of mint to nibble on as a digestif.

2 ounces Admiral Nelson's Spiced Rum
¾ ounce Lime Juice, freshly squeezed
¾ ounce Hibiscus Earl Grey Syrup*

2 dashes Angostura Bitters
Mint sprig, for garnish

Combine ingredients in a mixing glass with a small scoop of ice. Shake vigorously for 10 seconds, then strain over crushed ice in a lowball glass. Garnish with the mint sprig.

*Hibiscus Earl Grey Syrup: In a small sauce pot, add 1 cup water, ½ cup dried hibiscus flowers, and 2 bags Twining's Earl Grey tea. Bring the water to a simmer, and allow tea to steep for 2 minutes. Add 1 cup sugar, increase the heat and bring to a boil, stirring frequently. Once the liquid comes to a boil, turn the heat off, and steep for another 2 minutes. Strain the liquid, and allow to cool to room temperature.

Drifter's Daiquiri

Stephanie Teslar of Blue Hound Kitchen & Cocktails in Phoenix created this cocktail in honor of the release of Rhum Clément's Canne Bleue, an intensely aromatic high-proof rhum agricole from Martinique. "Agricole adds a nice rum funk from the blue cane stalk pressed to make this liquor," explains the mixologist, who adds spiced citrusy-sweet falernum with demerara and lime to complete a fresh, unique daiquiri.

1½ ounces Clément Canne Bleue
¾ ounce Velvet Falernum
¼ ounce Demerara Sugar

1 ounce Lime Juice, freshly squeezed
1 Mint sprig, for garnish

Combine ingredients in a mixing glass with cracked ice. Shake vigorously, and strain over crushed ice in a tiki mug. Garnish with mint sprig.

IRISH COFFEE

At the dawn of transatlantic air travel, flights from America regularly made stopovers at Port of Foynes in County Limerick, Ireland for refueling. On one night in 1942, a plane bound for the US was turned back to Foynes due to bad weather, and Joe Sheridan, head chef at the airport commissary, was instructed to prepare a strong, warming tonic for the group of stranded travelers. For each serving of strong black coffee, he added a shot of Irish whiskey, a spoonful of brown sugar, and a floating layer of lightly whipped heavy cream. The essence of the drink is diving through the cold cream to the warm underbelly. "It's such a pest to make, but never was such labor more richly rewarded," writes Kingsley Amis, the grand old man of English letters and self-proclaimed "one of the great drinkers, if not one of the great drunks, of our time."

Buena Vista Irish Coffee

Called "last of the old irreplaceables" by fellow columnist Herb Caen, Stanton Delaplane worked as travel writer for the *San Francisco Chronicle*. After discovering Irish coffee at the Shannon Airport in November of 1952, Delaplane returned home to San Francisco where he convinced Jack Koeppler and George Freeberg, owners of the Buena Vista Café, to replicate the drink. The secret is lightly whipped heavy cream—thick and frothy, but not stiff—floated over the whiskey-coffee mixture.

2 Sugar Cubes (or 2 teaspoons Sugar)
4 ounces Coffee, hot
1½ ounces Irish Whiskey
Heavy Cream, lightly whipped

Prepare an Irish coffee glass (or a wine glass or mug) by filling it with hot water. Discard hot water, and drop in sugar cubes (or sugar). Add hot coffee, and stir to dissolve sugar. Add Irish whiskey, and stir again. Gently ladle a collar of lightly whipped heavy cream to float on top of the drink.

Keoke Coffee

In 1966, George Bullington, a jockey agent at Santa Anita Racetrack, opened Bully's Restaurant in La Jolla, California. According to local legend, one night the restaurant staff was engaged in after-hours experimentation, when George created a coffee cocktail that became the restaurant's signature drink. It was called "George's Coffee" until one of the cooks, a Hawaiian, came up with the name that stuck: "Keoke" is Hawaiian for "George."

½ ounce Kahlúa
½ ounce Crème de Cacao
½ ounce Brandy
4 ounces Coffee, hot
Whipped Cream

Combine Kahlúa, crème de cacao, and brandy in a large mug or heat-resistant glass. Fill with hot coffee, leaving enough room for whipped cream.

Jamaican Coffee

In the 1950s, Doctor Kenneth Leigh Evans tasted a coffee-flavored liqueur, based on a recipe from the seventeenth century that had come down to family friends. He worked on recreating the drink in his lab, tinkering until he came up with the product that became Tia Maria. Jamaican Coffee was one of the cocktails that emerged as a result of the 1980s with the "dark spirit" TV ad campaign for Tia Maria featuring supermodel Iman, wife of British rock star David Bowie.

½ ounce Myer's Rum (or other Dark Rum)
1½ ounces Tia Maria
4 ounces Hot Coffee

Whipped Cream
3 coffee beans

Combine rum and coffee liqueur in a heat-resistant glass, and fill with hot coffee, leaving enough room for whipped cream. Garnish with coffee beans.

Iced Spanish Coffee

Portland, Oregon's oldest restaurant, Huber's Café, has been making dramatic coffee drinks since the early 1970s when mixologist James Kai Louie developed a signature version of the Spanish *carajillo*. Prepared tableside, with fire-filled theatrics, the iced version was created during an Oregon summer when guests began asking for ice in the drink. Huber's barman Alex Perez is called "the Baryshnikov of Spanish Coffee," serving as many as two hundred flaming coffees a day.

¾ ounce 151-proof Bacardi Rum
¼ ounce Triple Sec
2 ounces Kahlúa

Coffee, chilled
Whipped Cream, unsweetened
Grated Nutmeg, for garnish

In a small saucepan, combine the rum and triple sec, and ignite with a long match. Carefully add the Kahlúa, then pour the flaming mixture into an ice-filled pint glass. Add the coffee, top with the whipped cream, and dust with nutmeg.

Southern Limerick

At Pinewood Social, a gathering place in Nashville, Tennessee, cocktails are given the same thought and consideration as the food, in particular this Down South riff on Irish coffee—a sweet, savory concoction that warms you up with Guatemalan coffee, corn-based whiskey, and invigorating herbal liqueur.

¾ ounce James E. Pepper 1776 Rye
¾ ounce Meletti Amaro Liqueur
¼ ounce Demerara Simple Syrup + additional for whipped cream
Hot Coyegual Coffee
Demerara-sweetened Whipped Cream
Atomized Fee Brother's Old Fashioned Bitters

Combine rye, amaro, and simple syrup in a preheated Irish coffee glass. Add coffee, leaving enough room for whipped cream. Finish with a spray of atomized bitters.

Blind Abbot

A sixteenth-century Irish pirate and chieftain, Grace O'Malley has inspired musicians, novelists and playwrights to create works based on her adventures. She also inspired the bar mistresses at Grace's Bar in New York City, where Pam Wiznitzer invented a chilled rendition of Irish coffee.

1½ ounces Irish Whiskey
1 ounce Coffee, chilled
¾ ounce Galliano Ristretto
½ ounce Cinnamon Syrup*

3 dashes Angostura bitters
Whipped Cream
Ground Cinnamon, for garnish

Combine whiskey, coffee, liqueur, cinnamon syrup, and bitters in a mixing glass with cracked ice. Shake vigorously until outside of shaker is frosty, about 30 seconds. Strain into an Irish coffee glass, and top with whipped cream and cinnamon.

*Cinnamon Syrup: Bring 1 cinnamon stick, ⅓ cup demerara sugar, and ⅓ cup water just to a boil in a small saucepan, and remove from heat. Let stand 15 minutes. Strain syrup into an airtight container; cover, and chill.

Luciano

Bourbon deposes Irish whiskey in a not-so-subtle transformation of Irish coffee created by Chris Cardone behind the marble bar at White Street, the ultraplush New York City restaurant from chef Floyd Cardoz. The drink adopts its Italian attitude with a deep, dark espresso liqueur made in Italy—you know, where espresso was invented.

1¼ ounces Buffalo Trace Bourbon
¼ ounce Caffe Borghetti Espresso Liqueur
½ ounce Demerara Simple Syrup
2 dashes Fee Brothers Orange Bitters

4 ounces Hot Coffee
Whipped cream
Grated Nutmeg, for garnish

Combine bourbon, Caffe Borghetti, simple syrup and bitters into a tempered Irish coffee glass. Stir with a bar spoon to mix, and fill with hot coffee, leaving enough room for whipped cream. Dust with grated nutmeg over the top.

Sweet Love

Mixologist Lucy Brennan of Mint/820 appropriates ingredients from an obscure mixed drink called the Dirty Banana to create a bracing, Mexican-themed cocktail for those chilly winter nights in Portland, Oregon. Steaming hot coffee spiked with coffee-flavored liqueur and banana-flavored rum is perfectly matched with the coldest months of the year.

1 ounce Kahlúa
1 ounce Cruzan Banana Rum
3 ounces Hot Coffee
Whipped Cream
Mexican Chocolate, shaved, for garnish

Add liquid ingredients to a heat-resistant wine glass. Top with whipped cream, and dust with chocolate shavings over the top.

The Log Driver

Alison MacKenna and Sunny Yoanidis of The Gabardine in Toronto set out to create a boozy coffee with Canadian Club whisky and native maple syrup for, as they explain, "a true Canadian pedigree." The drink's name is an homage to "The Log Driver's Waltz," a school children's song about workers who "dance" on the logs as they float down rivers.

1½ ounces Canadian Club Whisky
½ ounce Maple Syrup
Espresso (or hot strong coffee)
Maple Whipped Cream*

Combine whisky and maple syrup in a rocks glass, and fill with coffee, leaving enough room for whipped cream. Serve on a saucer with a teaspoon.

*Maple Whipped Cream: Whip 1 cup heavy whipping cream with ¼ cup maple syrup until soft peaks form.

Café Foster

The dessert combination of rum and bananas first came together more than sixty years ago at Brennan's Restaurant in New Orleans. The Pembroke Room, nestled on the second floor of New York's Lowell Hotel, serves a dessert-inspired, dark rum– and banana liqueur–spiked, whipped cream–topped, hot coffee cocktail—the perfect counterpart to the legendary confection.

1½ ounce Bacardi Añejo Rum
¾ ounce Banana Liqueur
Hot Coffee
Whipped Cream
Cinnamon, for garnish

Combine rum and banana liqueur in a preheated Irish coffee glass. Fill with hot coffee, leaving enough room for whipped cream. Dust with cinnamon over the top.

Koffie Van Brunt

This hot coffee and rum cocktail gets its name from the Dutch word for coffee (*koffie*) and the street (Van Brunt) where it is served at St. John Frizell's Fort Defiance café-bar-neighborhood social center in Red Hook, Brooklyn. The bold character and smooth taste of Bacardi 8 (a blend of rums with an almost Scotch-like finish) mingles easily with espresso and black cherry liqueur—a perfectly acceptable way to start a cold winter day. Orange zest and nutmeg provide festive topper.

2 tablespoons Heavy Cream, chilled
1 ounce Bacardi 8-Year-Old Rum
½ ounce Cherry Heering
1 ounce Simple Syrup

1 shot Espresso (or 6 ounces strong black coffee)
Orange peel zest, finely grated, for garnish
Cinnamon, for garnish

Whisk cream in small bowl until slightly thickened but still pourable. Combine rum, Cherry Heering, and simple syrup in a warm mug. Add espresso. Float whipped cream, and dust with orange zest and cinnamon over the top.

Karl the Fog

Karl the Fog is a term San Francisco locals call the iconic gray fog that creeps in from the ocean. Inspired by the weather mascot as well as the city's Irish coffee legacy, Adam Jed created this cocktail at Fog City's Bluestem Brasserie. It's the local go-to drink when the clouds roll into town.

1 ounce Brandy
½ ounce Bénédictine
½ ounce Frangelico
½ ounce Kahlúa

Hot Coffee
Frangelico Whipped Cream*
Orange peel, for zest

Combine brandy, Bénédictine, Frangelico, and Kahlúa in a preheated Irish coffee glass. Add coffee, leaving enough room for whipped cream. Grate orange zest over the top.

*Frangelico Whipped Cream: Combine 1 cup heavy whipping cream with 2 ounces Frangelico in mixing bowl. Mix on high with electric mixer until whipped cream forms stiff peaks.

Irish Coffee Martini

At Finn McCool's in Southampton, New York, some like it cold. Irish coffee components are familiar, with coffee-flavored liqueur adding richness and depth to a drink that becomes a Martini when served in the classic, inverted-cone glass.

2 ounces Jameson Irish Whiskey
½ ounces Kahlúa Coffee Liqueur
3 ounces Coffee, chilled

½ teaspoon Brown Sugar + extra for garnish
Whipped Cream

Combine whiskey, Kahlúa, coffee, and sugar in a mixing glass with cracked ice. Shake vigorously, and strain into a chilled Martini glass. Add a dollop of whipped cream, and sprinkle brown sugar over the top.

Buena Vista Fizz

Irish coffee wasn't invented in San Francisco, but it was the warming potion's first stop in America. Although technically a variation on a classic fizz, this notion by Ian Scalzo of Tradition (The American Cocktail Bar) in San Francisco pays homage to the drink's local temple at the corner of Hyde and Beach Streets, the Buena Vista Café.

1 ounce Chicory-Infused Bulleit Rye*
1 ounce Jameson Irish Whiskey
½ ounce Lemon Juice, freshly squeezed
½ ounce Orange Juice, freshly squeezed

¾ ounce Coffee Syrup**
½ ounce Egg White
Club Soda, chilled
Cinnamon, for garnish

Combine ingredients in a mixing glass with cracked ice. Shake vigorously, and strain into an Irish coffee glass. Add a splash of club soda, and dust with cinnamon over the top.

*Chicory-Infused Bulleit Rye: Mix 6 ounces Bulleit rye and ½ tablespoon chicory in a resealable glass jar, seal, and shake well. Let infuse overnight, then fine-strain, and reseal.

**Coffee Syrup: Stir 2 tablespoons demerara sugar into 6 ounces of finely ground coffee until dissolved. Let cool before using.

The Matterhorn

The most famous peak in the world after Everest, the Matterhorn is a majestic rock that straddles the border between Switzerland and Italy. Its bone-chilling temperatures inspire a hot, Alpine herb-spiced cocktail, devised by Clint Rogers at The Dawson in Chicago, a loose play on the Irish coffee construct, replacing hot coffee with hot cocoa.

1½ ounces Génépy Des Alpes
1 ounce Punt e Mes
Hot Cocoa*
Woodruff Whipped Cream**
1 teaspoon Orange Zest, for garnish

Combine génépy and Punt e Mes in a warm mug. Add cocoa, leaving enough room for whipped cream. Garnish with orange zest over the top.

*Hot Cocoa: Combine 2 rounded teaspoons unsweetened cocoa powder and 1 rounded teaspoon sugar (or to taste). Warm 1 cup of milk in a small saucepan over medium heat until it is hot, not quite to a boil. Pour just enough of the hot milk into the cocoa-sugar mix, stirring to form a thoroughly combined paste, then add the remainder of the milk, and stir until completely incorporated.

**Woodruff Whipped Cream: Add 1 tablespoon dried woodruff leaves to 16 ounces of boiling water. Steep for 4 minutes. Strain liquid from leaves, add 16 ounces of sugar, and stir to dissolve. Let cool. Combine 1 cup heavy whipping cream with 2 ounces woodruff syrup in mixing bowl. Mix on high with electric mixer until whipped cream forms stiff peaks.

MANHATTAN

It's a sophisticated drink that embraces the energy of the place for which it's named. The Manhattan has a much-debated history, but everyone agrees the drink was indeed conceived in New York City in the second half of the nineteenth century. Attractive enough on their own, its ingredients become positively alluring when mixed, which explains the passion of devotees. While it's classically made with whiskey, sweet vermouth, and bitters, like its namesake, the Manhattan has always been adaptable. "Make no mistake about it," writes Lucius Beebe in *The Stork Club Bar Book*, "the Manhattan was the archetypal short mixed drink and blazed a trail for all others to follow."

Pierre's Manhattan

While the drink may have been created for Lady Randolph Churchill, Winston Churchill's mother, at the Manhattan Club in the 1870s, it was at Pierre's, on Forty-Fifth Street, immediately west of Fifth Avenue, where the Manhattan Cocktail was introduced to New York society. "Some connoisseurs or poseurs contend that in mixing a Manhattan cocktail, the whiskey must always be put into the mixing glass before the vermouth," writes Charles Brown in *The Gun Club Drink Book*, "but just why, deponent sayeth not."

2 ounces Rye Whiskey
1 ounce Sweet Vermouth
1 dash Angostura Bitters
Maraschino Cherry with stem, for garnish

Combine ingredients in a mixing glass with cracked ice. Stir briskly, and strain into a chilled cocktail glass. Garnish with cherry.

Saratoga Cocktail

In 1867, John H. Morrisey built the Club House Casino in Saratoga, New York, a gathering place for gamblers and card players like "Diamond Jim" Brady (and companion Lillian Russell), "Bet a Million" Gates, and bookie "Irish John" Cavanaugh. *New York World* reporter Nellie Bly once branded Saratoga "Our Wickedest Summer Resort." Popularized among the sporting crowd, the Saratoga Cocktail first appears in print in Jerry Thomas' 1887 *Bar-Tender's Guide*. (Although he calls for shaking with ice, the drink benefits from being stirred instead to preserve clarity.)

1 ounce Rye Whiskey
1 ounce Cognac
1 ounce Sweet Vermouth

2 dashes Angostura Bitters
Lemon peel, for garnish

Combine ingredients in a mixing glass with cracked ice. Stir briskly, and strain into a chilled cocktail glass. Express lemon peel over the glass, rub it around the rim, and drop it in.

Rob Roy

Invented in 1894 by a bartender at the Old Waldorf Men's Bar, the drink was named in honor of the premiere of *Rob Roy*, an operetta based upon Scottish folk hero Robert Roy MacGregor. Like the original Manhattan, a Scotch-based Rob Roy can be made with sweet, dry, or tempered with both sweet and dry vermouth, in which case the drink is called an "Affinity." Replace vermouth with Bénédictine in a Rob Roy, and you have yourself a "Bobby Burns." Contrast equal parts Scotch and sweet vermouth with blood orange juice and Cherry Heering, and you have yourself a "Blood & Sand" (named for the 1922 Rudolph Valentino film).

2 ounces Scotch Whisky
1 ounce Sweet Vermouth
1 dash Angostura Bitters
Maraschino Cherry with stem, for garnish

Combine ingredients in a mixing glass with cracked ice. Stir briskly, and strain into a chilled cocktail glass. Garnish with cherry.

Bobby Burns

A slight modification to the Rob Roy makes all the difference to a drink named after Robert Burns, the poet, balladeer, and Scotland's favorite son. "One of the very best Whisky Cocktails," writes Harry Craddock in *The Savoy Cocktail Book*. "A very fast mover on Saint Andrew's Day." Tradition holds that a shortbread cookie is served on the side.

2 ounces Scotch Whisky
1 ounce Sweet Vermouth
3 dashes Bénédictine

Combine ingredients in a mixing glass with cracked ice. Stir briskly, and strain into a chilled cocktail glass. Serve with a shortbread cookie.

Chancellor

Artifact of the late nineteenth or early twentieth century, the Chancellor is a sibling of the Rob Roy, the Scotch Manhattan, adding fruit-forward ruby port, and swapping dry vermouth for sweet. Scotch is called Scotch everywhere but Scotland—there it is merely referred to as whisky. The cocktail's name refers to the presiding officer of the Scottish Parliament. "If a dryer drink is wanted," wrote Charles Browne, "the use of French vermouth is allowable but is not orthodox."

2 ounces Scotch Whisky
1 ounce Ruby Port
½ ounce Dry Vermouth

2 dashes Orange Bitters
Orange peel, for garnish

Combine ingredients in a mixing glass with cracked ice. Stir briskly, and strain into a chilled cocktail glass. Express orange peel over the glass, rub it around the rim, and drop it in.

The Seelbach Cocktail

Inspired by European hotels in cities such as Vienna and Paris, the glitzy Seelbach Hotel opened in Louisville, Kentucky in 1905 and was soon regarded among the finest hotels in America. Throughout its long history, the Old Seelbach Bar has been frequented by many notables, including F. Scott Fitzgerald, who was once banned from the hotel bar after he had one too many. According to legend, this drink was invented "accidently" when a bartender used a customer's Manhattan to catch the overflow from a popped Champagne bottle.

1 ounce Bourbon
½ ounce Cointreau
3 dashes Angostura Bitters

4 dashes Peychaud's Bitters
Champagne, chilled
Orange peel, for garnish

Combine bourbon, Cointreau, and bitters in a mixing glass with cracked ice. Stir briskly, and strain into a chilled cocktail coupe glass. Top up with Champagne. Express orange peel over the glass, rub it around the rim, and drop it in.

Up-to-Date

Hugo Ensslin, head bartender at the Hotel Wallick in New York City, is credited with being the first to record recipes for a few classic cocktails, including the "Manhattan-esque" Up-to-Date in 1916's *Recipes for Mixed Drinks*, billed as "a complete list of the standard mixed drinks that are in use at present in New York City."

2 Dashes Grand Marnier
2 Dashes Angostura Bitters
1 ounce Sherry
1 ounce Canadian Club Whisky

Combine ingredients in a mixing glass with cracked ice. Stir briskly, and strain into a chilled cocktail glass.

~~~~~~

Brown University Cocktail

A simple, equal-parts bourbon and dry vermouth drink, the Rosemary Cocktail (dating to Mark Twain's "Gilded Age") was animated with a smidgen of orange bitters, courtesy of the Ivy Leaguers up in Providence—for good reason. That one seemingly subtle addition brings about an entirely different cocktail, not only in name but in taste. (For the Harvard version, switch to cognac and sweet Vermouth).

1½ ounces Bourbon Whiskey
1½ ounces Dry Vermouth
2 dashes Orange Bitters

Combine ingredients in a mixing glass with cracked ice. Stir briskly, and strain into a chilled cocktail glass.

Waldorf

It's one of the signature drinks of the original Waldorf, William Waldorf Astor's thirteen-story luxury hotel, opened in 1893 at the corner of Fifth Avenue and Thirty-Third Street. In his *The Old Waldorf-Astoria Bar Book*, A.S. Crockett calls for equal parts of whiskey, vermouth, and absinthe (too much absinthe for most tastes, so the recipe was modified over the years).

¼ ounce Absinthe, for rinse
2 ounces Rye Whiskey
¾ ounce Sweet Vermouth
2 dashes Angostura Bitters

Rinse a cocktail coupe glass with absinthe, and discard the excess. Combine remaining ingredients in a mixing glass with cracked ice. Stir briskly until chilled and diluted, and strain into the prepared glass.

Palmetto

While nearly all early versions of the Manhattan were whiskey-centric, white-jacketed Harry Craddock, one of the most influential bartenders of the early twentieth century, took a different path with the Palmetto, first appearing in *The Savoy Cocktail Book*. When Harry Craddock was asked about the proper way to consume a cocktail, he said, "Quickly. While it's still laughing at you."

1½ ounces Rum
1½ ounces Sweet Vermouth
2 dashes Orange Bitters
Orange peel, for garnish

Combine ingredients in a mixing glass with cracked ice. Stir briskly, and strain into a chilled cocktail glass. Express orange peel over the glass, rub it around the rim, and drop it in.

Scofflaw

In 1923, Delcevare King, a supporter of Prohibition, announced a $200 prize to anyone who created a term that best expressed "the idea of lawless drinker, menace, bad citizen." Over twenty-five thousand entries later, "scofflaw" was the winner, and the following year a bartender known only as "Jock," debuted his cocktail recipe at Harry's Bar in Paris. Poking fun at the folly of the American Prohibition, he called it the Scofflaw Cocktail. The formula first appeared in Patrick Gavin Duffy's 1934 *Official Mixer's Manual*. (Originally the Scofflaw was made with Canadian whisky, since production of American rye whiskey ceased during Prohibition).

1½ ounces Rye Whiskey
1 ounce Dry Vermouth
¾ ounce Lemon Juice, freshly squeezed
¾ ounce Grenadine
2 dashes Orange Bitters
Lemon peel, for garnish

Combine ingredients in a mixing glass with cracked ice. Shake vigorously, and strain into a chilled cocktail glass. Express lemon peel over the glass, rub it around the rim, and drop it in.

Marconi Wireless

It is said that the twentieth century didn't truly begin until December 12, 1901, when inventor Guglielmo Marconi succeeded in transmitting radio signals across the Atlantic. This recipe, essentially an Apple Brandy Manhattan, was supposedly named after the wireless genius himself, according to the *Old Waldorf-Astoria Bar Book,* on his visit to the hotel.

2 ounces Laird's Applejack
1 ounce Sweet Vermouth
2 dashes Orange Bitters
Orange peel, for garnish

Combine ingredients in a mixing glass with cracked ice. Stir briskly, and strain into a chilled cocktail glass. Express grapefruit peel over the glass, rub it around the rim, and drop it in.

Algonquin

The Algonquin Hotel on Forty-Fourth Street in New York City was headquarters to the legendary "Round Table," whose members included the likes of Dorothy Parker, Robert Benchley, George S. Kaufman, and Harpo Marx. They would gather for lunch, sip cocktails, exchange barbs, stories, anecdotes, and what have you—Prohibition be damned. In this liquid homage, the brawny shoulders of rye keep the sweetness of pineapple in check—and vice-versa.

1½ ounces Rye Whiskey
¾ ounce Dry Vermouth
¾ ounce Pineapple Juice

Combine ingredients in a mixing glass with cracked ice. Stir briskly, and strain into a chilled cocktail glass.

Remember the Maine

After the sinking of the *USS Maine* off the coast of Havana in 1898, war-mongering journalists used the phrase "Remember the *Maine*, to Hell with Spain" as a rallying cry that would jumpstart the Spanish-American War. "Treat this one with the respect it deserves, gentlemen," writes Charles H. Baker in his 1939 classic, *The Gentleman's Companion, or Around the World with Jigger, Beaker and Flask*. "Stir briskly in clock-wise fashion—this makes it sea-going, presumably!"

¼ ounce Absinthe
2 ounces Rye Whiskey
¾ ounce Sweet Vermouth
2 teaspoons Cherry Heering
Brandied Cherry, for garnish

Rinse a cocktail coupe glass with absinthe, and discard the excess. Combine remaining ingredients in a mixing glass with cracked ice. Stir briskly until chilled and diluted, and strain into the prepared glass. Garnish with cherry.

Stork Club Manhattan

After World War II, when New York City was the epicenter of American culture and the Stork Club was a key New York social institution, Lucius Beebe, author of *The Stork Club Bar Book*, wrote, "The most exciting Manhattan is one compounded with ordinary quality bar whiskey rather than the rarest overproof article. It is perhaps the only mixed drink where this generality obtains."

⅔ ounce Rye Whiskey
⅓ ounce Sweet Vermouth

Combine ingredients in a mixing glass with cracked ice. Stir briskly, and strain into a 3-ounce cocktail glass.

Occhi Marroni

They say things happen in Boulder that don't happen anywhere else. Case in point, the Occhi Marroni ("Brown Eyes"), created by Jodi McAllister at Frasca Food and Wine, a neighborhood restaurant inspired by the cuisine and culture of Friuli, Italy. Vermouth takes a back seat to amaro, and the resulting palate is quite unlike the standard Manhattan—less whiskey-driven, more bitter, and earthy as well as herbal.

1½ ounces Vanilla-Infused Rittenhouse Rye*
¾ ounce Amaro Montenegro
½ ounce Cocktail Punk Rose Vermouth
1 dash Cocktail Punk Morning Grapefruit Bitters
Grapefruit peel, for garnish

Combine ingredients in a mixing glass with cracked ice. Stir briskly, and strain into a rocks glass with 1 large cylindrical ice cube. Express grapefruit peel over the glass, rub it around the rim, and drop it in.

*Vanilla-Infused Rittenhouse Rye: Split 2 vanilla bean pods, and combine with 3 cups rye in airtight container. Let sit for 1 week. Strain before use.

Saint's Gallery

Think of this modern interpretation as an "inverted Scotch Manhattan," devised by Kenny Freeman at Julep in Houston, as whisky surrenders to Carpano Bianco (developed by Antonio Benedetto Carpano, the godfather of vermouth). Herbal Bénédictine, a spirit created by Benedictine monks five hundred years ago, speaks clearly to the aromatics.

1½ ounces Carpano Bianco Vermouth
¾ ounce Black Grouse Scotch
½ ounce Bénédictine
Absinthe, for rinse

Rinse a cocktail coupe glass with absinthe, and discard the excess. Combine remaining ingredients in a mixing glass with cracked ice. Stir briskly until chilled and diluted, and strain into the rinsed coupe.

In Cold Blood

Borrowing its name from the Truman Capote "nonfiction novel," this dark, blood-red libation was created by Andrew Volk at the Portland Hunt + Alpine Club. Over a strong rye base, Cynar lends bitter, vegetal notes with vermouth providing sweetness and aromatics. A mysterious and contemplative Manhattan prototype.

1 ounce Rye Whiskey
1 ounce Sweet Vermouth
1 ounce Cynar
Pinch of Salt
½ teaspoon Lemon Juice, freshly squeezed

Combine rye, vermouth, and Cynar in a mixing glass with cracked ice. Stir briskly, and strain into a chilled cocktail coupe glass. Finish with pinch of salt and squeeze of lemon.

The Smoking Jacket

Picture yourself in a red velvet smoking jacket, pipe in hand, sipping cocktails by the fireplace on a chilly autumn day. Okay, forget the pipe. At Toronto's County General, Jeremy Cheng extols the affinity between smoky bourbon and sweet maple syrup. Mixing the two amaros adds complexity, and standard Angostura is replaced by black walnut– and orange-flavored bitters. Flavors and aromas bleed into one another.

1½ ounces Bulleit Bourbon
½ ounce Averna Amaro
½ ounce Amaro Montenegro
1 teaspoon Maple Syrup

1 dash Fee Brothers Black Walnut Bitters
1 dash Regan's Orange Bitters
Orange peel, folded and pinned with Clove,
  for garnish

Combine ingredients in a mixing glass with cracked ice. Stir briskly, and strain into a rocks glass with 1 large cylindrical ice cube. Garnish with orange peel and clove.

Manhattan Nouveau

Perhaps more than most cocktails, the Manhattan can withstand the inevitable tinkering we've come to expect from the modern bar. There's no shortage of imaginative energy at Portand, Oregon's Little Bird, where Tom Lindstedt exploits the architecture of the classic, replacing traditional vermouth with a robust dry red wine, sweetened with luscious orange notes of Bénédictine.

2 ounces Old Grand Dad Bourbon
¾ ounce Château Buisson-Redon Bordeaux Rouge
½ ounce Bénédictine

Combine ingredients in a mixing glass with cracked ice. Stir briskly, and strain into a rocks glass with 3 medium ice cubes.

Improved Scofflaw

Sometimes evolution goes backward and forward. Chicago's Scofflaw takes its name from the term for a "lawless drinker" during Prohibition and the French cocktail that poked fun of "dry" America. Mixologist Meghan Konecny of Scofflaw redefines the boundaries of the original drink, replacing rye whiskey with Old Tom Gin while Cocchi Americano emerges to improve the complexity of the drink.

1½ ounces Scofflaw Old Tom Gin
½ ounce Cocchi Americano
½ ounce Grenadine
¾ ounce Lime Juice, freshly squeezed
Cucumber wheel, for garnish

Combine ingredients in a mixing glass with cracked ice. Stir briskly, and strain into a chilled cocktail coupe glass. Garnish with cucumber.

Whistle Blower

At the Gin Joint in Charleston, South Carolina, bar maestro Joe Raya applies his own creative spin to the Manhattan blueprint. Straight rye has a creamy texture, leaving notes of oranges, vanilla, and caramel to play across the palate, matching up with bitter-herbal amaro and lovely, chocolatey notes of crème de cacao in the well-made, balanced, and flavorful libation.

2 ounces Whistle Pig Rye
½ ounce Ramazzotti Amaro
¼ ounce Brown Crème de Cacao
2 dashes Angostura Bitters
Orange peel, for garnish.

Combine ingredients in a mixing glass with cracked ice. Stir briskly, and strain into a chilled cocktail glass. Express orange peel over the glass, rub it around the rim, and drop it in.

Deer Hunter

Often used to warm both body and soul on a chilly evening or to remedy a cold or flu, the preparation of a Hot Toddy can have many variations, including this brash, bourbon Manhattan-inspired rendering at San Francisco's West of Pecos, concocted by bottle slinger Brent Butler. The drink is bathed in the mellow, earthy sweetness of maple syrup.

1 bag Organic Chai Tea
½ ounce Buffalo Trace Bourbon
½ ounce Cardamaro
½ ounce Alvear Cream Sherry
½ ounce Maple Syrup
Cinnamon Stick, wrapped with Orange peel

Temper a toddy glass with hot water. Fill glass ⅔ full with hot water, add tea bag, and let steep for 2 minutes. Remove tea bag, add bourbon, Cardamaro, Sherry, and maple syrup, and stir to combine. Garnish with orange peel–wrapped cinnamon stick.

The Carpetbagger

For his modified Manhattan, Jayce McConnell of Edmund's Oast in Charleston, South Carolina employs Cocchi Torino, a fortified wine infused with flavorings of cocoa, rhubarb, and citrus. Averna, a member of the Italian amaro family of liquors, is sweet and moderately bitter, with a strong orange flavor, providing a mid-palate fullness that ties the robust and sophisticated drink together.

2 ounces Rittenhouse Rye
1 ounce Cocchi Torino
½ ounce Averna
3 dashes Angostura Bitters
2 dashes Bitter Truth Aromatic Bitters
1 dash Fee Brothers Whiskey Barrel Aromatic Bitters
3 Orange peels, to express

In a chilled coupe glass, express the oil from three peels of orange to coat the inside. Combine all ingredients in mixing glass. Stir briskly with ice until just chilled (do not over-dilute). Strain into the prepared glass.

First We Take Manhattan

"When creating a twist on a classic, especially one as iconic as the Manhattan," explains mixologist Erik Holzherr of Wisdom in Washington, DC, "it's important to respect the original recipe and history." In his vision of the cocktail (named for a Leonard Cohen anthem), rye is sweetened with a honey-infused bourbon and tickled with the botanicals of Chartreuse. "Vermouth becomes more prominent," says Mr. Holzherr, "as 'the glue' that binds all the flavors together."

1½ ounces Old Overholt Rye Whiskey
½ ounce Wild Turkey American Honey
   Bourbon
½ ounce Green Chartreuse
1 ounce Cinzano Red Vermouth
4 dashes Angostura Bitters

Combine ingredients (except bitters) in a mixing glass with cracked ice. Stir briskly, and strain into a chilled cocktail glass. Add bitters over the top.

Fig 'n Pig

Carnivores sink their teeth into Jay Foster's meaty twist on the Manhattan at Post 390 in Boston. At first sip, the cocktail appears subtle, but pay attention to the bacony flavor of the bourbon, caressed by fruit elements in the manner of an Old Fashioned. As the ice melts, the proof drops, and the salty, warm flavors change along with it. Each sip will be different. The ritual of making the drink is the fun part.

Candied Bacon Powder, for rim*
1 Lemon Wedge
1½ ounces Bacon-Infused Bourbon**
½ ounce Fig Purée***

¼ ounce Punt e Mes
3 dashes Orange Bitters
Long Orange twist, for garnish

Spread candied bacon powder on a small plate. Rub the rim of a tall glass with the lemon wedge, and dip rim in the powder. Add crushed ice to the glass; set aside. Combine bourbon, fig purée, Punt e Mes, and orange bitters in a mixing glass with cracked ice. Shake vigorously, and strain into prepared glass. Garnish with orange twist, meant to resemble a pig's tail.

*Candied Bacon Powder: Pre-heat oven to 400 degrees Fahrenheit. Arrange ½ pound thick-cut bacon on a sheet pan lined with aluminum foil. Place in oven, and bake until the bacon browns and the fat is rendered and bubbly, about 20 minutes. Remove bacon from the oven, brush with maple syrup, sprinkle with 3 tablespoons of brown sugar, and pat to adhere. Return to the oven, and bake until bacon is crisp, about 10 minutes. Let completely cool on a rack, then wrap in a cloth towel, and use a hammer to grind into a coarse powder.

**Bacon-Infused Bourbon: Combine 1½ ounces of bacon fat, 1 pinch of sea salt, 2 drops of liquid smoke in 750 ml bottle of bourbon, shake lightly, then lay bottle on its side at room temperature for 3 hours. Place in freezer for 2 hours (upside down if possible), then remove, and double strain with cheese cloth and coffee filter. Rinse out bottle to remove fat, and pour infusion back into clean bottle.

***Fig Purée: Combine 1 pint Black Mission figs (stemmed and halved), 1 tablespoon sugar, 2 tablespoons water, and 1 tablespoon fresh lemon juice in a blender and purée until smooth.

The Manhattan White Out

Mixologist (and Manhattan Cocktail devotee) Andrew Johnston of the storied Ryland Inn in Whitehouse Station, New Jersey, creates this winter notion of the classic tipple with Templeton White Rye, a Prohibition-era whiskey said to be gangster Al Capone's drink of choice. A solid formula with no weak links.

2½ ounces Templeton White Rye
1 ounce Carpano Bianco
2 dashes Orange Bitters
2 dashes Angostura Bitters
Grapefruit peel, for garnish

Combine ingredients in a mixing glass with cracked ice, and stir for a period of 10 to 15 seconds (40 to 50 revolutions) to ensure the proper dilution. Strain into a chilled cocktail coupe glass. Express grapefruit peel over the glass, rub it around the rim, and drop it in.

The Honolulu

His riff on the Manhattan cocktail, according to mixologist Michael Cadden of Tavern Law in Seattle, Washington, "starts with a vegetal apéritif that gives a slap of bitter aromatics up front. Then we get into the meat of it with bourbon's strong body and structure. After vermouth's bitter/sweet notes on the finish, lemon zest brings you to the front again, complementing the apéritif. You've come full circle."

½ ounce Salers Apéritif Gentiane Liqueur
2 ounces Heaven Hills Bonded 100-Proof Bourbon
½ ounce Punt e Mes

Combine ingredients in a mixing glass with cracked ice. Stir briskly, and strain into a chilled cocktail glass.

Cobble Hill

The cooling, fresh flavor of cucumber serenades in the background of vanilla and oak characters in the whiskey, as the amaro ramps up flavor profile. In the seasonal Manhattan, invented by Sammy Ross at New York's Milk & Honey, ripe citrus and mildly bitter notes are ever so faint on the finish. This is a nice drink to sip on a warm summer's day.

2 slices English Cucumber, peeled
2 ounces Rye Whiskey
½ ounce Dry Vermouth
½ ounce Montenegro Amaro
Lemon peel, to express oils

In a mixing glass, muddle the 1 cucumber slice. Add remaining ingredients, and stir with cracked ice to chill and dilute. Strain into a chilled cocktail coupe, and express lemon peel over the glass. Discard the spent peel, and garnish with the remaining cucumber slice.

Bourbon Bijou

An original-style Bijou dates back to Harry Johnson's *New and Improved Bartender Manual* published in 1900. Adam Robinson, mixologist at Park Kitchen in Portland, Oregon, replaces gin (a "jewel" in the vintage cocktail) with bourbon and goes on to prove that Chartreuse does indeed work with whiskey, if you give it a chance. The bitters medley provides balance and complexity.

2 ounces Bourbon
½ ounce Green Chartreuse
½ ounce Punt e Mes
1 dash Fee Brothers Orange Bitters
1 dash Regan's Orange Bitters No. 6

Combine ingredients in a mixing glass with cracked ice. Stir briskly, and strain into a chilled cocktail glass.

10 Dollar Smokin' Manhattan

Its simplicity has made the Manhattan something of a blank canvas for bartenders, whose variations go far beyond the basic. For an expressive Manhattan at the Carbon Bar in Toronto, mixologists are drawn to the idea of infusing a small-batch Canadian rye with sweet, succulent tobacco, adding an unexpected flavor profile that connects with the spirit's dark fruit and toasted oak.

2 ounces Tobacco-Infused Lot 40 Single Copper Pot Still Canadian Rye*
1 ounce Dolin Rouge Vermouth de Chambéry
5 dashes Angostura Bitters
Amarena Cherry, for garnish

Combine ingredients in a mixing glass with cracked ice. Stir briskly, and strain into a rocks glass with 1 large cylindrical ice cube. Garnish with cherry.

*Tobacco-Infused Lot 40 Single Copper Pot Still Canadian Rye: Add a pinch of Copenhagen long-cut dipping tobacco to a resealable glass container. Pour 1 pint of rye over the tobacco, and stir to loosen leaves. Seal the container, and set in a cool place overnight. Strain through a fine mesh sieve lined with cheesecloth.

Trail Mix

Dreamed up by Jon Navasartian of Church & State Bistro in Los Angeles, the drink is a play on the trail mix blend of fruit and nuts you might pack for an autumn hike. "It's dried orange and walnuts with a bourbon backbone," explains the mixologist, "and I thought it would be a perfect spirit-forward cocktail inspired by the season."

2 ounces Evan Williams Bourbon
¾ ounce Pierre Ferrand Dry Curaçao
¼ ounce Nux Alpina Nocino
Orange peel, for garnish

Combine bourbon, Curaçao, and Nocino in a mixing glass with cracked ice. Stir briskly, and strain into a rocks glass filled with fresh ice. Express orange peel over the glass, rub it around the rim, and drop it in.

MARTINI

Baltimore-born satirist H. L. Mencken called the Martini "the only American invention as perfect as the sonnet." The glass alone has become the universal symbol of cocktail culture. The earliest version of the celebrated cocktail was known as a Martinez, invented by "Professor" Jerry Thomas, bartender at the Occidental Hotel in San Francisco, sometime in the late 1850s or early 1860s. As the story goes, a prospector, preparing to set out for Martinez, California, put a gold nugget on the bar and asked Thomas to mix him up something special. The drink was dubbed the "Martinez" in honor of the customer's destination. Thomas's development of the drink, which first appeared in the 1887 edition of his *Bar-Tender's Guide*, is considered a precursor to the modern Martini.

Martinez

The Martini's earliest incarnation was shaped with Old Tom Gin, a botanically-intensive style, rounded by light sweetness. (Its interaction with sweet vermouth and maraschino actually suggests a kinship with the Manhattan cocktail). According to John Walker's *Bottoms Up: Being a Glossary of Useful Information for the Thirsty* (1928), George Rector's Hotel Claridge in New York City was a "turbulent rendezvous for the disciples of the Martinez."

1½ ounces Old Tom Gin
1½ ounces Sweet Vermouth
1 dash Angostura Bitters
2 dashes Maraschino Liqueur
Lemon peel, for garnish

Combine ingredients in a mixing glass with cracked ice. Stir briskly, and strain into a chilled cocktail coupe glass. Express lemon peel over the glass, rub it around the rim, and drop it in.

Turf Club

A sibling of the Martinez was first concocted at New York's Turf Club, the gentlemen's club on the corner of Madison Avenue and Twenty-Sixth Street, where members gathered to play the horses. Albert Stevens Crockett immortalized the thirst quencher in *The Waldorf-Astoria Bar Book*, writing, "At times a good half—possibly two thirds—of the crowd in the bar were interested in racing, and would appreciate a cocktail of such a name."

2 ounces Holland Gin (Genever)
1 ounce Sweet Vermouth
1 dash Angostura Bitters
Lemon peel, for garnish

Combine ingredients in a mixing glass with cracked ice. Stir briskly, and strain into a chilled cocktail coupe glass. Express lemon peel over the glass, rub it around the rim, and drop it in.

Gin and It

Bon vivant Charles H. Baker, who ate and drank his way around the world in the first quarter of the twentieth century, chronicled his adventure in the two-volume *Gentleman's Companion*. In it, he succinctly described the importance of gin: "No bar can be without dry gin and be called a bar." The "It" in this minimalist recipe is sweet (Italian) vermouth, "the wetter the better." The libation is sometimes called Gin and Cin (pronounced "sin") after Cinzano, a popular brand of Italian sweet vermouth. Traditionally, no ice is used in this drink; however, if you do mix over ice and add a dash of orange bitters, you'll have yourself a Yale Cocktail.

1½ ounces Gin
1½ ounces Sweet Vermouth

Combine ingredients in a mixing glass without ice. Stir and strain into a cocktail coupe glass.

Bronx

According to Magnus Bredenbek in *What Shall We Drink?* (1934), "The Bronx Cocktail, strange to say, was invented in Philadelphia, of all places! There it might have remained in obscurity had it not been for one Joseph Sormani, a Bronx restaurateur, who discovered it in the Quaker City in 1905." The Bronx Cocktail is essentially a "Perfect" Martini with a complement of orange juice.

2 ounces Gin
½ ounce Dry Vermouth
½ ounce Sweet Vermouth
1 ounce Orange Juice
Orange peel, for garnish

Combine ingredients in a mixing glass with cracked ice. Stir briskly, and strain into a chilled cocktail coupe glass. Express orange peel over the glass, rub it around the rim, and drop it in.

Zaza

A play by French playwrights Pierre Berton and Charles Simon, *Zaza* was produced in America in an 1898 adaptation by David Belasco. The title character is a prostitute who becomes a music hall entertainer and the mistress of a married man. Zaza captured the imagination of New York bartender Hugo Ensslin who included this appreciation in 1916's *Recipes for Mixed Drinks*.

1½ ounces Gin
1½ ounces Dubonnet Rouge
1 dash Angostura Bitters
Lemon peel, for garnish

Combine ingredients in a mixing glass with cracked ice. Stir briskly, and strain into a chilled cocktail coupe glass. Express lemon peel over the glass, rub it around the rim, and drop it in.

Hanky-Panky

The American Bar at London's Savoy Hotel was one of the early establishments to introduce American-style cocktails to Europe. Ada "Coley" Coleman became head bartender, where, during the 1920s, she mixed potions for the likes of Mark Twain, the Prince of Wales, Prince Wilhelm of Sweden, and Sir Charles Hawtrey. It was Hawtrey, Britain's leading comedy actor of the era, for whom Coleman created the Hanky-Panky cocktail.

1½ ounces Dry Gin
1½ ounces Sweet Vermouth
2 dashes Fernet Branca
Orange peel, for garnish

Combine ingredients in a mixing glass with cracked ice. Stir briskly, and strain into a chilled cocktail coupe glass. Express orange peel over the glass, rub it around the rim, and drop it in.

Cornell

In *The Old Waldorf-Astoria Bar Book*, Albert Crockett calls this drink "a compliment to an institution at Ithaca, many of whose alumni—mining engineers and others—used it to toast Alma Mater." If you splash in some orange bitters, the Cornell becomes a Dewey; if you add a squeeze of orange peel to a Dewey, you've got a Racquet Club, which, with sweet vermouth and a dash of Angostura, answers to the name of Hearst.

1½ ounces Gin
1½ ounces Dry Vermouth

Combine ingredients in a mixing glass with cracked ice. Stir briskly, and strain into a chilled cocktail coupe glass.

The Barry Cocktail

There's a strong tie between the Barry and other flirtations with the Martini formula during Prohibition, this version distinguished by a hint of mint. In 1929, Charles H. Baker, Jr. first met "Barry" at the Army & Navy Club in Manila, Philippines. Like all proper Martinis, according to Mr. Baker, the drink "must be cold indeed."

2 ounces Gin
1 ounce Sweet Vermouth
1 dash Angostura Bitters
½ teaspoon White Crème de Menthe

Add gin, vermouth, and bitters to a mixing glass with cracked ice. Stir briskly, and strain into a chilled cocktail coupe glass. Float crème de menthe by holding a teaspoon bottom-side-up over the glass and pouring the liqueur slowly over it.

Colony Cocktail

The Colony, rendezvous of New York high society, remained open through the "dry" years of Prohibition, hiding the liquor stash in an elevator as a precaution against raids by enforcement agents. Marco Hattem, the Colony's head bartender, is credited with not only devising the house cocktail, but while stirring Martinis was the nearly universal custom, he made a practice of shaking them vigorously.

1½ ounces Gin
¾ ounce Grapefruit Juice
2 teaspoons Maraschino Liqueur

Combine ingredients in a mixing glass with cracked ice. Stir briskly, and strain into a chilled cocktail coupe glass.

Satan's Whiskers

The cocktail emerged from the Embassy Club, a Hollywood speakeasy run by impresario Adolph "Eddie" Brandstatter. It is said that wherever Eddie was, that was the party. Satan's Whiskers is a variation on the Bronx, first appearing in print in Harry Craddock's *Savoy Cocktail Book* from 1930. (The drink can be made in two ways—either "straight" with Grand Marnier, or "curled" with orange Curaçao).

½ ounce Gin
½ ounce Grand Marnier
½ ounce Sweet Vermouth
½ ounce Dry Vermouth

½ ounce Orange Juice
1 dash Orange Bitters
Orange peel, for garnish

Combine ingredients in a mixing glass with cracked ice. Shake, and strain into a chilled Martini glass. Express orange peel over the glass, rub it around the rim, and drop it in.

Cooperstown

In *The Stork Club Bar Book*, Lucius Beebe imbeds this drink among the "less exotic but nonetheless popular noontime cocktails" served at the bar, a "perfect" version of the Martini, using equal parts of both sweet and dry vermouth. Skip the mint, and add a shot of Cognac for an Astor Painless Anesthetic, the Stork's hangover cure, devised by actress Mary Astor (Brigid O'Shaughnessy in *The Maltese Falcon*).

1½ ounces Gin
½ ounce Dry Vermouth
½ ounce Sweet Vermouth
2 sprigs Mint, for garnish

Combine ingredients in a mixing glass with cracked ice. Shake, and strain into a chilled Martini glass. Garnish with mint sprigs.

The Montgomery Martini

Charles Butterworth was one of the big screen's best comic eccentrics. In real life, he was Robert Benchley's drinking partner at the Garden of Allah in Hollywood where, after being dumped into the pool, he delivered the now-famous line: "I need to get out of these wet clothes and into a Dry Martini." By the 1940s, bartenders had begun to ease up on the vermouth. Named after British Field Marshal Bernard Montgomery, who liked to have a fifteen to one ratio of his own troops against enemy troops on the battlefield, the Montgomery Martini is fifteen parts gin to one part dry vermouth. In other words, just use a "vermouth rinse."

¼ ounce Dry Vermouth, for rinse
3 ounces Gin
Olive or Lemon peel, for garnish

Swirl vermouth around in a pre-chilled Martini glass until it is coated with the liquid, discard any excess. Add gin to a mixing glass filled with ice and stir. Strain into the prepared Martini glass. Garnish with olive or lemon peel.

Dirty Martini

In February 1945, when Franklin Roosevelt met with Joseph Stalin and Winston Churchill in Tehran, Iran to plan a second front against Nazi Germany, he served his favorite drink, a salty invention that adds olive brine to an otherwise standard Martini. (The brine should be added before the cocktail is shaken or stirred, not after it's poured into the glass). Extra olives are added to amplify the flavor.

2½ ounces Gin
½ ounce Olive Brine
¼ ounce Dry Vermouth
3 Olives, for garnish

Combine ingredients in a mixing glass with cracked ice. Stir briskly, and strain into a chilled Martini glass. Drop olives into the glass.

Souped-Up Gibson

The Gibson, improvised by bartender Charley Connolly of the Players Club for illustrator Charles Dana Gibson, creator of the "Gibson Girl," lends a whisper of savory to the Martini. In 1957, *Esquire* magazine compiled a list of celebrity thirst quenchers in *Drink Book*, including an onion-laden Gibson courtesy of Guy Lombardo, whose orchestra played at the Roosevelt Hotel in New York City.

2 ounces Gin
½ ounce Dry Vermouth
6 Pearl Onions, for garnish

Combine ingredients in a mixing glass with cracked ice. Stir briskly, and strain into a chilled Martini glass. Drop onions into the glass.

Vodka Martini

True Martini drinkers would never consider a Martini made with vodka to be a Martini, hence its original name, the Kangaroo. The vodka version first appeared in Ted Saucier's *Bottoms Up* in 1951. While the drink was a favorite of Dashiell Hammett, it was Ian Fleming's James Bond who did the most to popularize the drink when he uttered the famous line, "Vodka Martini, shaken, not stirred" in *Goldfinger*. When the cocktail is shaken instead of stirred, it "bruises" the gin, lifting the flavor, and breaks up more of the ice to make it colder. (The original name for a shaken Martini, now out of popular use, was a Bradford).

3 ounces Vodka
½ ounce Dry Vermouth
Olive or Lemon peel, for garnish

Combine ingredients in a mixing glass with cracked ice. Shake, and strain into a chilled Martini glass. Garnish with olive or lemon peel.

The Lucky Jim

In Kingsley Amis's *On Drink*, the grand old man of English letters devised this derivative of the Vodka Martini. "What you serve should be treated with respect," he writes, "not because it is specially strong but because it tastes specially mild and bland." For visual reasons, he suggests leaving the peel on the cucumber slice you float on top.

12 to 15 parts Vodka
1 part Dry Vermouth
2 parts Cucumber Juice
Cucumber slice, for garnish

Combine ingredients in a mixing glass with cracked ice. Shake and strain into a chilled Martini glass. Garnish with cucumber.

Julia Child Upside-Down Martini

Famous for popularizing French cuisine in the American kitchen, Julia Child improvised her own apéritif, essentially a Martini that's heavier on the vermouth than gin, closer in spirit to the way dry vermouth is consumed in Europe. Her recipe calls for a five-to-one ratio of Noilly Prat vermouth (her favorite) to gin, stirred with ice. As she said of her creation, "It's a nice refreshing drink. I usually have two."

2½ ounces Noilly Prat Vermouth
½ ounce Gin
Lemon peel, for garnish

In a white wine glass filled with ice, stir together gin and vermouth. Express lemon peel over the glass, rub it around the rim, and drop it in.

Margatini

It's a cross between a Martini and a margarita, invented during the early 1990s at Handsome Harry's in Naples, Florida. Tequila adds depth and spark while savory flavors of pineapple and pomegranate counteract tart, slightly bitter notes of the native, thin-skinned limes. Somerset Maugham declared that "Martinis should always be stirred, not shaken, so that the molecules lie sensuously one on top of the other." Harry doesn't agree.

2 ounces Tequila
1 ounce Pineapple Juice
1 ounce Pomegranate Juice
½ ounce Key Lime Juice
Key Lime slice, for garnish

Add ingredients to a mixing glass with cracked ice. Shake, and strain into a sugar-rimmed coupe. Garnish with key lime.

Earl Grey "Marteani"

Cocktail diva Audrey Saunders developed this modern classic at the Bemelmans Bar (named for author and illustrator of the *Madeline* series of children's books) in New York's Carlyle Hotel. Earl Grey tea provides nuances of apricot and tart orange to an elegant libation crafted with Tanqueray gin for its juniper-focused flavor and high proof.

¾ ounce Lemon Juice
1 ounce Simple Syrup
1½ ounces Earl Grey-Infused Tanqueray Gin*
1 Egg White
Lemon peel, for garnish

Combine ingredients in a mixing glass with cracked ice. Shake, and strain into a chilled Martini glass. Express lemon peel over the glass, rub it around the rim, and drop it in.

*Earl Grey-Infused Tanqueray Gin: Measure 4 tablespoons loose Earl Grey tea into 750 ml bottle of gin. Cap and shake, and let sit at room temperature for 2 hours. Strain through a fine sieve or coffee filter into a bowl. Rinse out bottle to remove loose tea, and pour infusion back into clean bottle.

Diana Ross

It resembles an inverted Martini, heavy on the apéritif and light on the gin, inspired by "Upside Down," the 1980 disco song by Ms. Ross. "All the ingredients are kept chilled," explains mixologist Alam Rivas, who perfected the cocktail at the Canvas Club in Brisbane, Australia, "and it's shaken for five seconds rather than stirred, which makes the flavors more delicate and aromatic."

2 ounces Lillet Rosé
¾ ounce Brokers 47% London Dry Gin
⅓ ounce Pêche de Vigne
Grapefruit peel, for garnish

Combine ingredients in mixing glass with cracked ice. Shake, and strain into a chilled Martini glass. Express grapefruit peel over the glass, rub it around the rim, and drop it in.

Pornstar Martini

The first version of a Pornstar Martini, concocted by London mixologist Douglas Ankrah, is tweaked for the regulars at Vesper, a small boutique bar in Amsterdam with a focus on artisan cocktails. As for the recommended drinking ritual, start with a bite of the passion fruit, sip the cocktail, and finish with the side of fizzy Prosecco to clean the palate.

1½ ounces Ketel One Vodka
1 ounce Boiron Passionfruit Purée
½ ounce Vanilla Syrup*
½ Passion Fruit shell, as garnish
Prosecco, chilled

Combine ingredients into a mixing glass with cracked ice. Shake, and strain into a chilled cocktail coupe glass. Float the passion fruit shell. Serve a shot of Prosecco on the side.

*Vanilla Syrup: Combine 1 cup sugar, 1 cup water, and 2 Madagascar vanilla beans in a small saucepan over medium heat, and stir until sugar dissolves. Remove from heat, and let cool to room temperature. Strain into a clean glass jar.

Martina

An elegant British brasserie and bar named in honor of the building's architect, The Gilbert Scott is located in the borough of St. Pancras, London. An evolving cocktail list, organized by mixologist Dav Eames includes an interpretation of the Martinez, early variant of the modern Martini, often described as a Manhattan made with gin instead of whiskey. Sweetness of vermouth fills the first sip; the swallow offers gin with bursts of cardamom and coriander, intermixed with notes of ripe peach.

1½ ounces Opihr Oriental Spiced Gin
¾ ounce Sweet Vermouth
½ ounce Bols Peach Liqueur
2 dashes Angostura Bitters
Orange peel, for garnish

Combine ingredients in a mixing glass with cracked ice. Stir briskly, and strain into a chilled Martini glass. Express orange peel over the glass, rub it around the rim, and drop it in.

Susan Sontag

Dedicated to the woman who wrote about the intersection of high and low art, this spirit-forward abstract work from Grandma's Bar in Sydney, Australia, has the elegance of a Martini, with dramatic brushstrokes of mezcal, restrained floral hues, and undertones of ripe peach "brightened" with Peychaud's.

1½ ounces Del Maguey Vida Mezcal
1½ ounces Dolin Bianco Vermouth
1 dash Créme de Pêche
2 dashes Peychaud's Bitters
Lemon peel, for garnish

Combine ingredients in a mixing glass with cracked ice. Stir briskly, and strain into a chilled Martini glass. Express lemon peel over the glass, rub it around the rim, and drop it in.

Bambi Warhol

In Ian Fleming's *Casino Royale*, published in 1953, secret agent James Bond orders his dry Martini with both gin and vodka, a drink later named the Vesper. At Artusi in Seattle, Washington, where Jason Stratton's passion for cocktails falls within the Italian palate, his dalliance with Mr. Bond's Martini anchors gin and vodka with an Italian aperitivo of fortified Moscato d'Asti steeped with bitters and citrus.

1½ ounces Aviation Gin
¾ ounce 360 Vodka
¼ ounce Cocchi Americano
1 dash Scrappy's Orange Bitters
Orange peel, for garnish

Combine ingredients in a mixing glass with cracked ice. Stir 30 to 40 times or until the mixture is extremely cold. Strain into a chilled Martini glass. Express orange peel over the glass, rub it around the rim, and drop it in.

Frontier Medicine

Showman P. T. Barnum said, "There's a sucker born every minute," prompting a post-Prohibition bartender to create a cocktail called Barnum Was Right, a successful partnership of gin and brandy. At The Huguenot in New Paltz, New York, Derek Williams refines the herbal aspects of gin and fruity sweetness of cognac for a lovely drink with a trifle of citrus tart for balance.

2 ounces Prairie Gin
1 ounce Fevrier Cognac
4 dashes Reagan's Orange Bitters
Orange peel, for garnish.

Combine ingredients in a mixing glass with cracked ice. Stir briskly, and strain into a chilled snifter glass. Express orange peel over the glass, rub it around the rim, and drop it in.

Breakfast Martini

Once upon a time, cocktails were considered a morning drink—a bracer against the forthcoming day. Jams and marmalades appeared in cocktails, including one called the Marmalade Cocktail, listed in *The Savoy Cocktail Book* of 1930. At London's One Lombard Street, a brasserie and circular bar directly opposite the Bank of England, tea-infused gin is flavored with the richness of orange marmalade and the orange expression of Cointreau. Serve with buttered toast on the side.

1½ ounces English Breakfast Tea–Infused Langley's No. 8 Distilled London Gin*
¾ ounce Cointreau
2 teaspoons Orange Marmalade
¾ ounce Lime Juice, freshly squeezed
Orange peel, for garnish

Combine infused gin, Cointreau, lime juice, and marmalade in a mixing glass with cracked ice, and shake vigorously (to break up marmalade and mix it with the liquid ingredients). Fine-strain into a chilled Martini glass. Express orange peel over the glass, rub it around the rim, and drop it in.

*English Breakfast Tea–Infused Langley's No. 8 Distilled London Gin: Measure 4 tablespoons loose English Breakfast tea into 750 ml bottle of gin. Cap and shake, and let sit at room temperature for 2 hours. Strain through a fine sieve or coffee filter into a bowl. Rinse out bottle to remove loose tea, and pour infusion back into clean bottle.

La Perle de Mer

Perched on the fortieth floor of the Heron Tower, Duck & Waffle is the highest restaurant in the UK. Looming over London, the establishment's bar program, developed by Richard Woods, has made its presence known to those below with eccentric, indulgent cocktails. Reimagining the classic, Mr. Woods adds salty/savory notes to a Vodka Martini, infusing vermouth with oyster shells for a whisper of salinity and lovely mineral characters.

2 ounces Grey Goose Vodka
½ ounce Oyster-Infused Noilly Prat Dry Vermouth*
1 raw Oyster, for garnish

Combine ingredients in a mixing glass with cracked ice. Stir briskly, and strain into a chilled Martini glass over the raw oyster.

*Oyster-Infused Noilly Prat Dry Vermouth: Add 8 oyster shells to a sealable container, and cover with the contents of a 750 ml bottle of vermouth. Leave to rest for 24 hours. Filter through a coffee filter, and reserve until needed.

The Riverdale

Memories of An Beal Bocht, an Irish pub in the Bronx neighborhood of Riverdale, provided sentimental inspiration to Patrick McDonald after he landed at Central Provisions in Portland, Maine. The Riverdale is a Bronx Cocktail spinoff, swapping Irish whiskey for gin and invigorating with Orange Bitters.

1½ ounces Paddy's Irish Whiskey
½ ounce Cocchi Vermouth di Torino
½ ounce Dolin Dry Vermouth
½ ounce Orange Juice, freshly squeezed
2 dashes Regan's Orange Bitters No. 6
Orange peel, for garnish

Combine ingredients in a mixing glass with cracked ice. Shake, and strain into a chilled Martini glass. Express orange peel over the glass, rub it around the rim, and drop it in.

Bananas Foster Martini

It's part of the culinary culture of New Orleans. As a dessert, the luscious dish was hatched in 1951 at legendary Brennan's Restaurant. The creamy combination of bananas and rum is transformed into a cocktail at another Brennan family restaurant, Ralph's on the Park, where it's called a "Martini" and is strained into a Martini glass—but it's still decadent enough to serve as dessert.

1½ ounces Absolut Vanilla Vodka
1 dash Spiced Rum
1 ounce Créme de Banana
½ ounce Butterscotch Schnapps
1 splash fresh Cream
Nutmeg, for garnish

Combine ingredients in a mixing glass with cracked ice. Shake, and strain into a chilled Martini glass. Dust with nutmeg.

The Big Daddy Martini

While the gin and dry vermouth prototype will always remain *the* Martini, practically any concoction poured into that swanky, conical, stemmed glass can now have "-tini" affixed to the end of its name. Inspired by Chef Kent Rathbun (Iron Chef America winner and four-time James Beard Award nominee) and served at his restaurants, Abacus and Jasper's in Dallas, The Big Daddy is actually a light, refreshing, citrus-forward vodka sour in disguise.

1 ounce Grey Goose L'Orange Vodka
1 ounce Grey Goose Le Citron
¼ ounce Triple Sec
¼ ounce Simple Syrup

½ ounce Sweet and Sour Mix*
Orange slice, for garnish
Lemon slice, for garnish

Combine ingredients in a mixing glass with cracked ice. Shake vigorously, and strain into a chilled Martini glass. Garnish with orange and lemon.

*Sweet and Sour Mix: Combine 1 cup of sugar, 2 cups of water, and 2 cups of fresh lemon juice. Dissolve sugar in the water, and add the lemon juice.

◇◇

Breakfast of Champions

Cocktails are often a mark of simultaneous frivolity and finesse. The Wheaties cereal slogan provides inspiration to Seth Sempere of Seattle's Spur Gastropub. And, like the waitress in Kurt Vonnegut's classic novel of the same name, bartender Bonnie MacMahon declares "Breakfast of Champions" each time she delivers the bitters-soaked Martini to a patron.

2 ounces Copperworks Gin
1 ounce Dolin Blanc Vermouth
2 light dashes Regan's Orange Bitters
2 light dashes Scrappy's Grapefruit Bitters

1 pinch of Salt
Lemon peel, to express
Grapefruit peel, for garnish

Combine ingredients in a mixing glass with cracked ice. Stir briskly, and strain into a chilled Martini glass. Express lemon and grapefruit peels over the glass and drop them in.

NEGRONI

As ingredients for cocktail compositions go, it would be hard to argue against the significance of Campari. Formulated in 1860 by Gaspare Campari, the owner of a café in Novara, Italy, the secret blend of herbs and fruit, originally called "Bitter Uso Olanda," was devised as an apéritif beverage. The most famous Campari-based cocktail was first concocted around 1920 at the Caffé Casoni in Florence, when Count Camillo Negroni asked bartender Luca Picchi to add a shot of gin to his Americano. One of the earliest reports of the drink came during a 1947 visit to Florence by Orson Welles who so described the Negroni: "The bitters are excellent for your liver, the gin is bad for you. They balance each other." The Negroni formula has become a jumping off point for many other bitter drinks.

Americano

Without the Americano, there would not be a Negroni. Dating back to the 1860s, the bittersweet drink was first called a Milano-Turino, for Milan and Turin, home cities of the primary ingredients. During Prohibition, the Italians dubbed it the "Americano" for its popularity among American expats. The spicy, herbal, and deliciously bitter flavor of Campari shines through in this heady cocktail.

1 ounce Campari
1 ounce Sweet Vermouth
Splash of Club Soda
Orange slice, for garnish

Build in a rocks glass with ice. Stir to combine. Garnish with orange slice.

Caffé Casoni Negroni

The mystical union of Campari, sweet vermouth, and gin (the "Holy Trinity" of cocktail ingredients) was conceived and popularized at the Caffé Casoni in Florence's famed Palazzo Strozzi, a hub of Anglo-Florentine sophistication during the interwar years. The venerable Italian concoction is built with a traditionally simple yet powerful recipe, an interplay between sweet, bitter, and sour components.

1 ounce Gin
1 ounce Campari
1 ounce Sweet Vermouth
Orange slice, for garnish

Build in a rocks glass with ice. Stir to combine. Garnish with orange slice.

The Boulevardier

Among the literary expatriates of 1920s Paris, Erskine Gwynne began publishing the *Boulevardier*, a magazine patterned after the *New Yorker*. Gwynne, a nephew of the Vanderbilt family, was a frequenter of Harry's New York Bar and the twenty-seventh member of the "Barflies," an organization for serious drinkers with its own secret handshake and a necktie featuring a fly on a lump of sugar. The drink composed for and named after the magazine can be considered the Jazz-Age bastard child of the Manhattan and the Negroni.

1 ounce Bourbon
1 ounce Sweet Vermouth
1 ounce Campari
1 Orange Slice, for garnish

Build in a rocks glass with ice. Stir to combine. Garnish with orange slice.

Old Pal

William Robertson, nicknamed "Sparrow," was the sports editor of the *New York Herald* and a man who was known to call even those he'd just met, "Old Pal." This formula appears in the appendix of Harry McElhone's 1927 *Barflies and Cocktails*, introduced in Robinson's own words: "Here's the drink I invented when I fired the pistol the first time at the old Powderhall foot races."

1 ounce Canadian Whisky
1 ounce Dry Vermouth
1 ounce Campari
Orange peel, for garnish

Combine ingredients in a mixing glass filled with cracked ice. Stir briskly until well chilled, and strain into a chilled cocktail coupe glass. Express orange peel over the glass, rub it around the rim, and drop it in.

Lucien Gaudin

Winner of the Coupe d'Honneur at the 1929 French Professional Barmen's Championship, this "Frenchified" riff on the Negroni was named for one of the great classical fencers of the twentieth century. It swaps sweet vermouth for dry in a kind of hybrid between the Negroni and Martini, with the orange-flavored liqueur sweetening the dry vermouth.

1 ounce Gin
½ ounce Campari
½ ounce Cointreau
½ ounce Dry Vermouth
Orange peel, for garnish

Combine ingredients in a mixing glass filled with cracked ice. Stir briskly until well chilled, and strain into a chilled cocktail coupe glass. Express orange peel over the glass, rub it around the rim, and drop it in.

The Cardinale

This translation of the Negroni is believed to have originated in the Excelsior Hotel on the Via Veneto in Rome, Italy, sometime in the 1930s. The hotel was immortalized in Federico Fellini's *La Dolce Vita*, and the cocktail, in its own way, is a pledge of allegiance to the sweet life. (*Mr. Boston: Official Bartender's Guide* includes the Negroni-inspired recipe called Rosita, with tequila in place of gin and equal measures of sweet and dry vermouth.)

1½ ounces Gin
1½ ounces Campari
1½ ounces Dry Vermouth
Lemon peel, for garnish

Build in a double rocks glass with ice. Stir to combine. Express lemon peel over the glass, rub it around the rim, and drop it in.

Sbagliato

The Negroni Sbagliato (or "Negroni Gone Wrong") was concocted in the 1960s at Bar Basso in Milan during what should have been the mixing of a standard Negroni. An apprentice may have switched bottles around, so when bartender Mirko Stocchetto grabbed what would normally be gin, a bottle of sparkling wine was in his hand. This "happy accident" produced a cocktail embraced by those who prefer a more easily quaffable drink. Note: Do not insult the Prosecco with abusively vigorous stirring.

1½ ounces Sweet Vermouth
1½ ounces Campari
1½ ounces Prosecco (or other sparkling wine), chilled
Orange slice, for garnish

Build in a double rocks glass with ice, adding Prosecco last. Garnish with orange slice.

War and Peach

The original Negroni prescription rewards variation. This departure, formulated by Ben Speak and Jessie Pottinger at the Black Sparrow Lounge & Drinkery in Wellington, New Zealand, is a case in point. It's a sweeter style yet tempered by the savory element of sage. (Locals make these with New Zealand's own Rogue Society or Lighthouse Gin).

1½ ounces Gin
1½ ounces Rinquinquin Pêche Liqueur
1½ ounces Aperol
Fresh Sage leaves, for garnish

Add ingredients to a rocks glass or tumbler with ice and 1 or 2 sage leaves. Stir to combine. Garnish with sprig of sage.

The Thin Man

The series of *Thin Man* films are permeated with drinking scenes. Nick and Nora Charles (played by William Powell and Myrna Loy), a sophisticated, glamorous, pleasure-seeking, and urbane husband-wife detective team, are honored by mixologists at Craft & Commerce in San Diego, California. Citrus provides perfect counterpoint to Campari's unrelenting bitterness.

½ ounce Lemon Juice, freshly squeezed   ½ ounce Campari
1 ounce Grapefruit Juice, freshly squeezed   1½ ounces Hendrick's Gin
½ ounce Simple Syrup   Club Soda, chilled

Combine ingredients (except soda) in a mixing glass with cracked ice. Shake vigorously, and strain over new ice in a Collins glass. Top up with a float of club soda.

Blonde Negroni

Recipes are meant to be reexamined, and the Negroni just simply begs for deviation. Bar manager, Johnny Schaefer of Moxie Kitchen + Cocktails in Jacksonville, Florida dabbles with gentian root liqueur as a stand-in for Campari and a pale, dry-style apéritif for traditional vermouth. It's light, clean, and floral—a perfect summertime adaptation of the standard.

1 ounce Spring 44 Gin
1 ounce Lillet Blanc
¾ ounce Suze Liqueur
Lemon peel, flamed, for garnish*

Combine ingredients in a mixing glass with cracked ice. Stir for 10 seconds, and strain over 1 large cylindrical ice cube in an Old Fashioned glass. Garnish with flamed lemon peel.

*Flamed Lemon Peel: Warm a coin-shaped slice of peel over a lit match. Holding the peel between forefinger and thumb and taking care not to drop it, snap fingers sharply and strongly to press out oil quickly, releasing it into the cocktail. Rub the peel around the rim of the glass. Drop the twist into the drink or discard.

Ruby Red Negroni

The vast high-ceilinged dining room is flanked by two marble-topped bars at The Hamilton in Washington, DC, where cocktails put the focus on small-batch American spirits. Loosely based on the classic Negroni, this drink includes Vermont gin distilled from local grain with juniper, then sweetened with local honey. With grapefruit juice replacing sweet vermouth, it's more refreshing, slightly bitter, and easy to sip on a summer afternoon.

1½ ounces Barr Hill Gin
½ ounce Campari
1 ounce Ruby Red Grapefruit Juice
Grapefruit peel, for garnish

Combine ingredients in a mixing glass, and stir briskly until well chilled. Strain over new ice in a rocks glass. Express grapefruit peel over the glass, rub it around the rim, and drop it in.

Negroni's Evil Twin

Aperol becomes an adulteress, ousting Campari as the bedrock of this rogue Negroni served at Jack's Bistro in Baltimore, Maryland. Although they are both Italian apéritif liqueurs, and both bright red, Campari and Aperol are indeed different. Considered a gentler cousin to Campari, Aperol is sweeter, has less alcohol, and is slightly less bitter. Elderflower liqueur allows more of the gin flavors to shine through; lime keeps it from becoming too cloying.

1 ounce Aperol
1 ounce St. Elder Natural Elderflower Liqueur
1 ounce Small's Gin
½ ounce Lime Juice, freshly squeezed
Lime peel, for garnish

Combine ingredients in a mixing glass with cracked ice. Shake vigorously, and strain over new ice in a tumbler. Express lime peel over the glass, rub it around the rim, and drop it in.

Mona Lisa

A quenching Negroni rendition, exotic and yet somehow familiar, is fashioned by Richard Vargas at 4th & Swift in Atlanta. While gin and (a restrained) Campari remain the usual suspects, a bitter and aromatic apéritif stands in for vermouth. Mr. Vargas adds a soft, "painterly" texture with cognac-based pear liqueur while mezcal works its smoky-spicy magic.

¼ ounce Del Maguey Crema de Mezcal,
    for rinse
1¾ ounces Plymouth Gin
¼ ounce Campari

½ ounce Cocchi Americano Rosa
½ ounce Belle de Brillet
1 dash 18.21 Earl Grey Bitters
Lemon peel, for garnish

Rinse a cocktail coupe glass with mezcal and discard the excess. Combine remaining ingredients in a mixing glass with cracked ice. Stir briskly until chilled and diluted, and strain into the prepared glass. Express lemon peel over the glass, rub it around the rim, and drop it in.

Clarendon Boulevardier

Kyle Jahn of the Liberty Tavern in Arlington, Virginia, wraps his composition around the vintage Whiskey Negroni, with bourbon standing in for gin. The spinoff is an alluring, after-dinner sipper built with Kentucky straight bourbon, tamed with the placid sweetness of Dolin Rouge, and armed with a bitter, herbaceous blast courtesy of Fernet Branca.

Orange peel, to express
4 drops Fernet Branca
1½ ounces Old Forester Bourbon

¾ ounce Dolin Rouge
½ ounce Campari

Express orange peel (with as little pith as possible) over fresh ice in a rocks glass. Place peel on top of ice with the pith side down, and run 4 drops of Fernet over the sweet side of the peel into the ice. Add remaining ingredients to a mixing glass with cracked ice. Stir, and strain over the orange peel in the prepared glass.

West Coast Negroni

At 515 Kitchen & Cocktails in Santa Cruz, California, mixologist Ethan Samuels shuffles ingredients of the original formula, resulting in a cross between a Negroni and a Shandy. According to Mr. Samuels, "the components highlight hop flavors in the IPA—pine with the gin, lemon citrus with the grapefruit bitters, and resinous bitterness with the Campari—light and quenching with a bitter finish."

½ ounce Junipero or St. George Terroir Gin
½ ounce Campari
½ ounce Lemon Juice, freshly squeezed
½ ounce Simple Syrup

2 dashes Scrappy's Grapefruit Bitters
2½ ounces hoppy West Coast–style IPA
Lemon wedge, for garnish

Combine ingredients (except the IPA and lemon wedge) in a mixing glass with cracked ice. Shake vigorously, and strain into a tumbler with new ice. Top up with IPA. Garnish with lemon wedge.

Indecent Proposal

Michael McCollum echoes the spirit of the vintage Boulevardier at New York's Pouring Ribbons, balancing a rich, intense vermouth with the bitter notes of Cynar and amaro—mixing with the assertive rye for seductive palate complexity. "I wanted to brighten the drink so I added mint to the mixing glass," explains Mr. McCollum. "It's incredibly bright, comforting, and smooth for something involving so many bold ingredients. It looks like a winter drink (dark), reads like a winter drink (heavy ingredients), but is accessible for any time of year."

1 ounce Rittenhouse Rye
½ ounce Cynar
½ ounce Nardini Amaro

¾ ounce Cocchi Vermouth Di Torino
1 Mint sprig + 1 for garnish
Lemon peel, to express

Combine liquid ingredients and 1 mint sprig in a mixing glass. Very lightly press mint, to gently extract oils. Add ice, and stir briskly until well chilled. Double-strain into rocks glass with 1 large cylindrical ice cube. Express lemon peel into drink and discard. Garnish with spanked mint sprig.

Crime in Vatican City

Bartenders Dominik Aschauer and Tony Migliarese cut a gentler tack at the Cilantro Restaurant in Calgary, Alberta, Canada. Their Negroni adaptation relies on a complex rush of orange-flavored liqueur and creamy almond syrup. It's a testament to the power of Campari that it actually can compete for attention with a mere dusting. Not nearly as strong as some of its liquor-heavy counterparts, it's criminally refreshing.

1 ounce Bombay Gin
1 ounce Cocchi Americano Vermouth
½ ounce Cointreau
½ ounce Orgeat Syrup

1 ounce Egg White
¼ ounce Lemon Juice, freshly squeezed
Dehydrated Campari Powder, for garnish*

Combine ingredients in a mixing glass (except the Campari powder), and dry shake. Add ice to shaker, and shake vigorously. Double-strain into chilled Martini glass. Dust with dehydrated Campari.

*Dehydrated Campari Powder: Pour enough Campari to cover the bottom of a small baking sheet. Place in a 170-degree Fahrenheit oven, and bake for 12 hours. The Campari will eventually lose its water and alcohol, solidifying. Scrape the solid Campari "brick" off the baking sheet; crush it into a powder.

Gimme Shelter

Sprezzatura, the Italian word for "nonchalance," is perhaps the quality that best defines the versatile Negroni. One of the most unexpected variants of the classic model involves subbing the traditional gin for a blended malt whisky and vermouth for Lillet Rouge—performed with a certain nonchalance at the McCarren Hotel + Pool's Sheltering Sky in Brooklyn.

1 ounce Monkey Shoulder Scotch
1 ounce Campari
1 ounce Lillet Rouge
Grapefruit peel, for garnish

Combine ingredients in a mixing glass, and stir briskly until well chilled. Strain over new ice in a rocks glass. Express grapefruit peel over the glass, rub it around the rim, and drop it in.

The New Black

Barkeep John Ginnetti at 116 Crown in New Haven, Connecticut, assembles this blackcurrant liqueur-spiked Negroni with a new ingredient and a playful name. Cassis adds a persistent and inviting bouquet, as fruit flavors combine with bitters, botanicals, and citrus to create a sensation on the palate. The color is evocative of sunlight going down and turning from day to night.

1 ounce G. E. Massenez Crème de Cassis
¾ ounce Campari
¾ ounce Martin Miller's Gin

¾ ounce Lime Juice, freshly squeezed
1 handful Mint (orange mint is preferred)
Club Soda, chilled

Hold mint in the palm of one hand, and slap it with the other to break the capillaries. Drop into a mixing glass, add all ingredients (except soda) with cracked ice, and shake vigorously. Pour all into a double rocks glass, and top up with a float of club soda.

Negroni Flip

Mixologists at the Social Kitchen & Bar in Birmingham, Michigan pitch the standard on its head. "Traditionally, a Negroni is an acquired taste that balances the bitterness of Campari, the sweetness of the vermouth, and the complexity of gin," explains Michael Gray. "We wanted to make it more approachable with a palate-pleasing creaminess and sweetness, so we added egg whites for froth and replaced Campari with Aperol, the less bitter 'little sister.'"

1 ounce Hendrick's Gin
1 ounce Aperol
1 ounce Sweet Vermouth

¼ ounce Simple Syrup
1 Egg White
Orange peel, for garnish

Combine ingredients in a mixing glass with cracked ice, adding the egg last. Shake vigorously for about 20 seconds. Strain through a fine-mesh strainer into a cocktail coupe glass. Express orange peel over the glass, rub it around the rim, and rest on top of the foam.

OLD FASHIONED

The earliest cocktails consisted merely of sugar, bitters, water, and a spirit of choice. By the mid-nineteenth century, new-fangled recipes began to appear, to the dismay of traditionalists. Eventually, gentlemen began to ask bartenders for cocktails in the "old fashioned" way, those simple mixes of spirits, sugar, bitters, and water. In 1889 (and possibly as late as 1895), head bartender Martin Cuneo of Louisville, Kentucky's Pendennis Club formalized a drink recipe in honor of Colonel James E. Pepper, club member and local bourbon distiller, and attached a name that stuck—Old Fashioned. It is said that he introduced it to the staff of the Men's Bar at the Waldorf Hotel in Manhattan, providing its gateway to the world. (An essential ingredient, Angostura was first compounded in 1824 by Dr. Johann Siegert to soothe stomach maladies and nausea). About muddling, Charles Browne (*Gun Club Drink Book*) wrote, "It does seem rather a rude way to treat good whiskey, but the ladies seem to like it."

Pendennis Club Old Fashioned

It's the original formula—a balance between booze and sweet, fruity and bitter—and it represents an essential chapter in cocktail history. While a family of drinks can be called Old Fashioned, made from any spirit (1930's *The Art of Drinking* includes a gin Old Fashioned), the Pendennis Club set the whiskey standard. The gentlemen of Louisville also set the standard for service, requiring a specific "rocks" glass—appropriately, the Old Fashioned glass.

1 teaspoon Simple Syrup
½ slice Orange
1 Cherry with stem

1 Lemon twist
2 dashes Angostura Bitters
2½ ounces Kentucky Bourbon

Combine first five ingredients in a traditional Old Fashioned glass. Muddle with a wooden pestle, then add 1 or 2 cubes of ice and bourbon. Stir to chill.

Old Fashioned Whiskey Cocktail

"Taken sanely and in moderation, whiskey is beneficial, aids digestion, helps throw off colds, megrims, and influenzas," writes Charles Baker in *The Gentleman's Companion*. "Used improperly the effect is just as bad as stuffing on too many starchy foods, taking no exercise, or disliking our neighbor." Head bartender "Colonel" Jim Gray was convinced that, with the passing of the Fifth Avenue Hotel, "there won't be a place on earth left where a gentleman can get an old fashioned whiskey cocktail." He provided this recipe to a *New York Sun* reporter in 1908, and insisted, "For heaven's sake, no bitters."

2 ounces Bourbon or Rye Whiskey
1 sugar cube
Nutmeg

Muddle sugar cube, a teaspoon of water, and a sprinkle of nutmeg in a mixing glass. Add the whiskey. Shake with ice, and strain the drink into an Old Fashioned glass.

Whiskey Cocktail

"Serious-minded persons omit fruit salads from Old Fashioneds," insists Crosby Gaige in his *Cocktail Guide and Ladies' Companion*, "while the frivolous window-dress the brew with slices of orange, sticks of pineapple, and a couple of turnips." Apparently, Harry Craddock agrees. In *Barflies and Cocktails*, published in Paris in 1927, he offers the drink stripped to its bones, with sweetened syrup providing a silky texture, full mouthfeel, and weightier texture.

1 teaspoon Simple Syrup
3 dashes Angostura Bitters
Orange peel, for garnish
2 ounces Scotch or Rye Whiskey

In a small bar glass, combine simple syrup and bitters. Fill glass halfway with ice, then stir about a dozen times. Add enough ice to fill glass. Squeeze orange peel over glass to extract oils, add peel to glass, and add whiskey.

Dixie Whiskey Cocktail

It's the very picture of tradition as burnished over slabs of mahogany, yet the Old Fashioned has never been a product of exacting process. This variation, which first appeared in Tom Bullocks's 1919 *The Ideal Bartender*, was standardized by Harry Craddock in *The Savoy Cocktail Book* a decade later. Kingsley Amis provided advice for making an Old Fashioned: "You really have to use bourbon. The Rye Old Fashioned is not too bad; the Irish version just tolerable; the Scotch one not worthwhile."

2 ounces Bourbon
2 lumps Sugar
½ teaspoon Lemon Juice, freshly squeezed

½ teaspoon Orange Curaçao
½ teaspoon Angostura Bitters
2 teaspoons White Crème de Menthe

Add ingredients to a mixing glass half-filled with ice. Shake carefully. Pour (do not strain) into an Old Fashioned glass.

Delmonico's Old Fashioned

It was New York's first grand restaurant, owned by the Delmonico family, who opened locations all over the city, one on Beaver Street, one on Madison Avenue, William Street, and Fifth Avenue. A booklet prepared by the Angostura-Wuppermann Company in 1934 includes the following Old Fashioned recipe as mixed by Agosto Forte at Delmonico's:

> Crush ½ lump of sugar in 5 or 6 dashes of Angostura bitters, and shake around glass so as to coat it with sugar grains and bitters. Empty balance of the mixture. Add pieces of pineapple, orange, and a cherry. Lump of ice. Jigger of rye whiskey. Splash with seltzer, and serve.

New Fashioned

After swimming in obscurity for several decades, the Old Fashioned began to regain fame after the end of World War II, and by the 1960s, Americans had fallen back in love with the drink. (The Old Fashioned is the cocktail of choice of Don Draper, the lead character on the *Mad Men* television series, set in the 1960s). Service of this version at various golf clubs in Northern California signaled the resurgence of this grand old cocktail, reclaiming the potion like the discovery of a lost artifact.

4 fresh Basil Leaves
2 Strawberries
1 Sugar Cube
1 dash Angostura Bitters

2 ounces Bourbon
1 ounce Sweet Vermouth
1 splash Club Soda, chilled

In a pint glass, muddle fresh basil, 1 strawberry, sugar, and bitters. Add ice along with bourbon and vermouth, and gently stir to mix and chill. Pour (do not strain) into an Old Fashioned glass. Add splash of club soda and garnish with remaining strawberry.

Old Pepper

"This drink is nothing for children to toy with," cautions Charles Baker in *The Exotic Drinking Book* volume of *The Gentleman's Companion* (1939), "but for action and plenty of it we report that little is lacking on that score." He recommends serving in "any sort of fireproof glass."

1½ ounce Rye Whiskey
1 ounce Lemon Juice, freshly squeezed
½ teaspoon Worcestershire

½ teaspoon Chili Sauce
3 drops Tabasco
¾ ounce Bourbon

Combine ingredients in a mixing glass with cracked ice. Shake, and strain over crushed ice in an Old Fashioned glass.

Old Fashioned Vanilla

Bar Chef Mike Hernandez imagines this contemporary variation as a winter tipple at The Woolworth Restaurant and Cocktail Bar in Dallas, pairing the aromatics of vanilla and cinnamon with a bold rye whiskey. "I decided to keep the flavors separate," he explains, "allowing each of them to shine at different stages throughout the cocktail."

¼ ounce Vanilla Simple Syrup*
2 ounces Old Overholt Rye Whiskey
2 dashes Angostora Bitters
Cinnamon Stick, for garnish

Combine ingredients in a mixing glass with cracked ice. Shake, and strain into an Old Fashioned glass with 1 large spherical ice cube. Garnish with cinnamon stick.

*Vanilla Simple Syrup: Bring ½ cup raw sugar and ½ cup brown sugar with 1 cup water to a boil in a saucepan over medium heat, and simmer, stirring, for about 20 minutes. Let cool completely. Stir in 1½ teaspoons pure vanilla extract.

Honey Mash

Honey provides sweet, fragrant floral notes and a touch of warmth to an Old Fashioned, as mixologists at the Mash Bar in Ann Arbor, Michigan employ a single ingredient to ensure the counterbalance of honey and bourbon. The bourbon-spiked honey liqueur puts the focus on the sweetener but not so heavily as to overwhelm the whiskey's cinnamon and oak notes.

1½ ounces Bärenjäger Honey & Bourbon
2 fresh Strawberries
2 slices fresh Orange + 1 slice for garnish
Club Soda, chilled

Muddle berries and 2 orange slices in the bottom of a mixing glass. Add bourbon and ice. Shake vigorously, and strain into a rocks glass with new ice. Top with float of club soda, and garnish with remaining orange slice.

Levinson's Old Fashioned

There's the Chrysler and the Empire State, but the Empire Diner in the city's Chelsea neighborhood is more quintessentially New York than just about any other building. That's where Todd McMullen and David Kleinman came up with a variant on the Old Fashioned for a favored patron. Rye makes the drink sharper and less sweet, in addition to being the traditional nineteenth-century whiskey of choice.

2 ounces Old Overholt Rye Whiskey
½ ounce Averna Amaro
⅛ ounce Allspice Dram
2 dashes Angostura Bitters

1 dash Orange Bitters
Lemon peel, for garnish
Orange peel, for garnish

Add ingredients in an Old Fashioned glass with ice. Stir to combine. Express both lemon and orange peels over the glass, rub them around the rim, and drop them in.

Eberson's Old Fashioned

Architect John Eberson was best known for extravagantly designed movie palaces in the 1920s, including the Tampa Theatre, a jewel in the cultural landscape of West Florida. At Datz, the popular Tampa gastropub where bacon is the signature ingredient, Summer Perez devised an "Old Fashioned" tribute to the talented Mr. Eberson. Vermouth adds herbal notes that are missing from a traditional Old Fashioned.

2 Amarena Cherries
¼ ounce Lemon Juice, freshly squeezed
½ ounce Simple syrup
2–3 dashes Fee Brothers Old Fashioned Bitters

2 ounces Buffalo Trace Bourbon
1 ounce Dolin Vermouth Rouge
Club Soda, chilled
Candied Bacon*

In a rocks glass, muddle cherries with lemon juice, sugar, and bitters. Add the bourbon, vermouth, and ice. Stir to combine. Top with float of club soda and skewer of candied bacon.

*Candied Bacon: Brush with water, then coat both sides of a medium cut slice of bacon with brown sugar. Skewer bacon in a zig zag pattern and bake until desired crispness.

Brigham Young Fashioned

Salt Lake City's Pallet Bistro names its Old Fashioned-inspired cocktail for the city's founder, who built his own whiskey distillery—for medicinal purposes only (of course). Mixologist Bijan Ghiai's signature remedy is a flamboyant affair, compounding a pair of bourbons with an array of bitters and the essence of orange from a dash of Grand Marnier.

½ teaspoon Raw Sugar
4 dashes Angostura Bitters
1 dash Regan's Orange Bitters
1½ ounces Bulleit Bourbon

½ ounce Maker's Mark Bourbon
½ ounce Ramazotti Amaro
1 dash Grand Marnier
Orange peel, for garnish

Add sugar to an Old Fashioned glass. Wet with the bitters, and muddle with a wooden pestle. Add the bourbons, amaro, and Grand Marnier. Add one or two large ice cubes, and stir to chill. Express orange peel over the glass, rub it around the rim, and drop it in.

Toronto

It's a significant departure, to be sure, but it stays close enough to the trodden trail of the original to warrant consideration as an after-dinner Old Fashioned. Max Toste of Deep Ellum in Allston, Massachusetts, employs Fernet Branca for a pungent, creamy bite. It doesn't upstage the other ingredients but adds a mosaic of flavors that slowly change with each sip. The lemon zest is a must as it helps to brighten up an otherwise dark drink.

2 ounces Rye Whiskey
½ ounce Simple Syrup
½ ounce Fernet Branca

1 dash Angostura Bitters
Lemon peel, for garnish

Add ingredients to a mixing glass with cracked ice. Stir briskly until well chilled, and strain into a rocks glass with one large spherical ice cube. Express lemon peel over the glass, rub it around the rim, and drop it in.

The Bearded Lady

"The perfect cocktail will take you on a journey," says Michelle Ruocco of The Bent Brick in Portland, Oregon. "After you smell, sip, and swallow, you should still be detecting flavors and experiencing the drink." Her Bearded Lady is a shrub-style Old Fashioned with a good healthy dose of bitters to cut sweetness and round out the flavor.

1 ounce Strawberry Shrub*
2 ounces Temperance Trader Bourbon
2 teaspoons Black Pepper Syrup**
Pinch of Salt
15 dashes Angostura Bitters

Combine ingredients in a mixing glass with cracked ice. Shake vigorously, and double-strain into large cocktail coupe glass.

*Strawberry Shrub: Hull and chop enough strawberries to fill 2 quart containers. Place strawberries in large cambro or other storage container. Add 2 quarts of sugar, and mix thoroughly until combined. Let sit in refrigerator 2 days, stirring well each day. On the third day, add 2 quarts red wine vinegar, and mix well to combine. Let sit 2 more days, stirring well each day. Strain mixture through cheesecloth placed in sieve, and let drain 30 minutes. Squeeze cheesecloth to expel any extra liquid, then discard cheesecloth and its contents. Keep refrigerated.

**Black Pepper Syrup: Combine 1 cup black peppercorns and 3 cups vodka in airtight container. Shake well, and let sit overnight. Strain through sieve, and add 2 ounces simple syrup. Mix thoroughly. Store in an airtight container in a cool, dark place.

Attorney Privilege

Orgeat (pronounced "or-zsa," like Zsa Zsa Gabor) is an almond syrup, usually reserved for tropical cocktails, yet in the hands of Erick Castro of Polite Provisions in San Diego, it becomes an aromatic sweetener in an energetic play on the classic. The whiskey, which tastes of sweet chocolate and spicy rye, takes the law into its own hands.

2 ounces Buffalo Trace Bourbon
½ ounce Orgeat Syrup
2 dashes Angostura Bitters
Lemon peel, for garnish

Combine ingredients in a mixing glass with cracked ice. Stir briskly until well chilled. Strain into a cocktail coupe glass. Express lemon peel over the glass, rub it around the rim, and drop it in.

Apple Old Fashioned

From its origins, the Old Fashioned has expanded to countless variations on a timeless theme, usually with fruit as an integral part of the drink. In autumn, mixologist Jeremy Wilson at Portland, Oregon's Ned Ludd introduces the essence of apples to his rendering of the classic. A large, spherical ice cube, which adds to the beauty of the drink, keeps it satisfactorily chilled and yet refrains from the sin of dilution.

2 ounces Elijah Craig 12-Year-Old Bourbon
½ ounce Apple Simple Syrup*
2 dashes Angostura Bitters

1 dash Fee Brothers Old Fashioned Bitters
Lemon peel, for garnish

Combine ingredients in a mixing glass with cracked ice. Stir, and strain into a rocks glass with 1 large spherical ice cube. Express lemon peel over the glass, rub it around the rim, and drop it in.

*Apple Simple Syrup: Peel and chop 1 whole Granny Smith apple. In a small saucepan, combine chopped apple with 1 cup of white sugar, 1 cup brown sugar, 1 cinnamon stick, a pinch of salt, and 1½ cups of water. Bring to a boil, then reduce to a simmer, and continue to simmer for 1 hour. Let cool, then strain.

Petit Cochon

The Old Fashioned cocktail has inspired countless odes and imitations over the last hundred or so years. At Chez Moi, a French bistro nestled within a Brooklyn storefront, bacon "fat-washed" rye becomes the signature component in a savory rendition on the classic, one that hits all the right notes: smoky without being overwhelmed with the notes of bacon, elegant but also adventurous.

1 teaspoon Demerara Sugar
1 dash Angostura Bitters
2 dashes Woodford Reserve Cherry Bitters

½ Orange Wheel
1 Maraschino Cherry, stemless
2 ounces Bacon-Infused Rye*

Add sugar to an Old Fashioned glass. Wet with the bitters, add orange and cherry, and muddle with a wooden pestle. Add the infused rye and 1 large cylindrical ice cube.

*Bacon-Infused Rye: Combine 1½ ounces of bacon fat, 1 pinch of sea salt, 2 drops of liquid smoke in 750 ml bottle of rye. Shake lightly, then lay bottle on its side at room temperature for 3 hours. Place in freezer for 2 hours (upside down if possible), then remove, and double strain with cheese cloth and coffee filter. Rinse out bottle to remove fat, and pour infusion back into clean bottle.

Nutty Old Fashioned

Esquire magazine insists the "manliest cocktail" is an Old Fashioned with no fruit. They didn't say anything about nuts. Wood-paneled walls and beach-house tchotchkes set the stage at Son of a Gun in Los Angeles for Daniel Warrilow's take on the old standby, calling on savory walnut liqueur for complexity and soda-soaked demerara sugar as a sort of "smoothing agent." The predominant flavor is still that of the whiskey, as you slowly sip your way down its length.

1 teaspoon Demerara Sugar
Club Soda, chilled
1½ ounces Bulleit Bourbon

½ ounces Nux Alpina Walnut Liqueur
Orange peel, for garnish

Muddle the sugar with splash of soda in an Old Fashioned glass. Add bourbon and walnut liqueur to an Old Fashioned glass with 1 large spherical ice cube. Stir to combine. Express orange peel over the glass, rub it around the rim, and drop it in.

Earl Grey Old Fashioned

Spirits, bitters, and sugar. An Old Fashioned is the sum of these parts, in perfect balance, and nothing more. At the Lowry in Minneapolis, Minnesota, mixologist Colin Weaver dresses up the spirit with fragrant tea and adds just enough sweetener and bitters to give the drink boxing gloves, if you will.

2½ ounces Earl Grey Tea–Infused
    Rye Whiskey*
½ ounce Simple Syrup

2 dashes Angostura Bitters
2 dashes Bittercube Cherry Bark Vanilla Bitters
Lemon peel, for garnish

Combine ingredients in a mixing glass, and stir with cracked ice. Strain into a chilled cocktail coupe glass. Express lemon peel over the glass, rub it around the rim, and drop it in.

*Earl Grey Tea–Infused Rye Whiskey: Measure 4 tablespoons loose, Earl Grey tea into 750 ml bottle of rye. Cap, shake, then let sit at room temperature for 2 hours. Strain through a fine sieve or coffee filter into a bowl. Rinse out bottle to remove loose tea, and pour infusion back into clean bottle.

⬦⬦⬦

Oaxacan Old Fashioned

Robert Simonson, who writes about cocktails for the *New York Times*, called this drink "the most renowned of the twenty-first-century variations of the Old-Fashioned, and one of the modern cocktail's gateway drinks into the pleasures of tequila and mezcal." Conceived by Phil Ward at New York's Death & Co., tequila and mezcal take over the leading role that bourbon plays in the immortal Old-Fashioned, with agave nectar playing the sweetener role. A flamed orange peel with toasted essential oils is the proverbial cherry on top of this masterpiece.

1½ ounces El Tesoro Reposado Tequila
½ ounce Vida Mezcal
1 teaspoon Agave Nectar

2 dashes Angostura Bitters
Orange peel, flamed, for garnish*

Combine ingredients in a mixing glass with cracked ice. Stir, and strain into a rocks glass with 1 large spherical ice cube. Garnish with flamed orange peel.

*Flamed Orange Peel: Warm a coin-shaped slice of peel over a lit match. Holding the peel between forefinger and thumb and taking care not to drop it, snap fingers sharply and strongly to press out oil quickly, releasing it into the cocktail. Rub the peel around the rim of the glass. Drop the twist into the drink or discard.

WHISKEY SOUR

According to a 1946 article in *Gourmet Magazine*, "The sour is a bar benchmark, a bit like roast chicken at a French bistro or a scoop of vanilla at the ice cream parlor." Most historians attribute the invention of the citrus-flavored cocktail to Elliot Stubb, a steward aboard the British merchant ship *Sunshine*. After settling in the then-Peruvian port city of Iquique in 1872, Stubb opened a bar where he became fascinated with the possibilities of the *limón de pica*—a small lime grown in the area. One fine day, he mixed blended whiskey with the juice of the local lime and a dose of sugar for a drink he dubbed the sour. Over the years, mixologists have discovered that many other base spirits respond well to this basic template.

Ward 8

It happened in Boston back in 1898 at Locke-Ober, a gathering place central to the financial, political, and cultural history of Beantown. A bartender by the name of Tim Hussion concocted an early interpretation of the sour in honor of political boss Martin B. Lomasney from the city's Ward 8 who had just won a seat in the state legislature—in spite of the fact that Lomasney didn't drink and was a staunch Prohibitionist.

2 ounces Rye Whiskey
½ ounce Lemon Juice, freshly squeezed
½ ounce Orange Juice, freshly squeezed

1 teaspoon Grenadine Syrup
Maraschino Cherry, for garnish

Combine ingredients in a mixing glass filled with cracked ice. Shake vigorously, and strain into a cocktail coupe glass. Garnish with cherry.

∞∞

Pisco Sour

An American from Salt Lake City, Victor Morris traveled to Peru to work as a cashier for the rail line that served ore mining in the Cerro de Pasco district. In 1915, he moved to Lima, and a year later opened Morris' Bar, a haunt for local swells and well-heeled tourists. During the 1920s, one of his bartenders, Mario Bruiget, tweaked the sour formula, adding pisco, a spirit produced by distilling wine from the Pisco Valley near the coast. His drink became the country's national cocktail.

3 ounces Pisco
1 ounce Simple Syrup
1 ounce Lime Juice, freshly squeezed

1 Egg White
3 dashes Angostura Bitters, for garnish

Combine ingredients in a mixing glass filled with cracked ice. Shake vigorously, and strain into a cocktail coupe glass. Sprinkle Angostura bitters on top of the foam.

The Aviation

Created by Hugo Ensslin, head bartender at the Hotel Wallick in New York, and first published in Ensslin's 1916 *Recipes for Mixed Drinks*, the recipe is a variation on the gin sour, using maraschino as sweetener. Although the drink originally called for a dash of crème de violette, the obscure liqueur was omitted in Harry Craddock's influential *Savoy Cocktail Book* (1930).

2 ounces Gin
2 teaspoons Maraschino
¾ ounce Lemon Juice, freshly squeezed

Combine ingredients in a mixing glass filled with cracked ice. Shake vigorously, and strain into a cocktail coupe glass.

Jack Rose

Its name is a play on words: the drink is made with apple*jack* and is *rose*-colored from the grenadine. (Applejack is a calvados-style apple brandy, which has claims to being the oldest American spirit due to its roots in the colonial period). The fruity, spirit-forward drink appears in Ernest Hemingway's 1926 classic, *The Sun Also Rises*, in which Jake Barnes, the storyteller and protagonist, drinks a Jack Rose at the bar of the Hôtel de Crillon while awaiting the arrival of Lady Brett Ashley.

2 ounces Laird's Applejack
1 ounce Lemon Juice, freshly squeezed
½ ounce Grenadine

Combine ingredients in a mixing glass filled with cracked ice. Shake vigorously, and strain into a cocktail coupe glass.

Clover Club

Christened for the Philadelphia Men's Club whose members gathered at the Bellevue-Stratford Hotel, and according to the *Old Waldorf-Astoria Bar Book*, "dined and wined, and wined again." The Clover Club drinker was described by Jack Townsend, president of the Bartenders Union of New York and author of *The Bartender's Book*, as "traditionally a gentleman of the pre-Prohibition school," a "distinguished patron of the oak-paneled lounge."

2 ounces Gin
Juice of ½ Lemon
1 teaspoon Grenadine
1 Egg White

Combine ingredients in a mixing glass filled with cracked ice. Shake vigorously, and strain into a small wine glass.

Southside Cocktail

Jack and Charlie's '21' Club was designed with its own disappearing bar and a secret cellar to hide the illegal liquor from prying eyes, and although the speakeasy was raided by police numerous times during Prohibition, not a drop of alcohol was ever found. The Southside Cocktail is said to have been invented at the Southside Sportsmen's Club on Long Island, then popularized by the '21' faithful. The cocktail is sometimes topped with Champagne to make a Southside Fizz.

2 ounces Gin
1 ounce Lemon Juice, freshly squeezed
¾ ounce Simple Syrup
Sprig of fresh Mint

Combine ingredients in a mixing glass filled with cracked ice. Shake vigorously, and strain into a cocktail coupe glass. Garnish with mint sprig.

White Lady

In the first decades of the last century, several new-born and quite distinct cocktails were called "White Lady," yet the one that survived, a gin-based confection, is credited to Harry Craddock of the Savoy, his recipe published in the *Savoy Cocktail Book* (1930). Joe Gilmore, former head barman at The Savoy, said this was a favorite drink of Stan Laurel and Oliver Hardy.

1½ ounces Gin
¾ ounce Cointreau
¾ ounce Lemon Juice, freshly squeezed

Combine ingredients in a mixing glass filled with cracked ice. Shake vigorously, and strain into a cocktail coupe glass.

Pink Lady

Lady Mendl, 1930s society figure and author of the influential book *The House in Good Taste*, is thought to be responsible for the popularity of the Pink Lady. The drink differs from the Clover Club only with the addition of apple brandy. A New Orleans version replaces egg white with a dollop of cream for a Pink Shimmy.

1½ ounces Gin
1 teaspoon Laird's Applejack
1 teaspoon Lemon Juice, freshly squeezed
1 teaspoon Grenadine
1 Egg White

Combine ingredients in a mixing glass filled with cracked ice. Shake vigorously, and strain into a cocktail coupe glass.

Sidecar

Through the 1930s, the Ritz Bar was the first port of call in a city teeming with American expats in search of a drink. Without doubt, the bar became one of the most select watering holes in the world, and Frank Meier, the drink-shaker-in-charge, burnished a reputation for inventive cocktails, including the Sidecar, allegedly created to cool down a Ritz regular who always arrived on a motorcycle with a sidecar. (In 1934, *Burke's Complete Cocktail & Drinking Recipes* suggested sugaring the rim of a Sidecar glass).

1½ ounces Brandy
¾ ounce Cointreau
¾ ounce Lemon Juice, freshly squeezed

Combine ingredients in a mixing glass filled with cracked ice. Shake vigorously, and strain into a cocktail coupe glass.

Improved Sidecar

In 1933, just after the repeal of Prohibition, Julien J. Proskauer compiled a "not too dry text book about cocktails" called *What'll You Have?* He proposed improving Frank Meier's Sidecar by boosting the orange-sweetness and substituting tropical rum for brandy.

1½ ounces Bacardi Rum
1½ ounces Cointreau
¾ ounce Lemon Juice, freshly squeezed

Combine ingredients in a mixing glass filled with cracked ice. Shake vigorously, and strain into a cocktail coupe glass.

Rattlesnake

The Savoy Cocktail Book claims "it will either cure a rattlesnake bite, or kill rattlesnakes, or make you see them." Dating back to the original 1930 publication of the bartending manual from London's Savoy Hotel, this sour-style cocktail is just the right harmony of sweet and sour, with frothy airiness provided by an egg white.

1½ ounce Blended Whiskey
1 teaspoon Lemon Juice, freshly squeezed
¼ teaspoon Absinthe
½ teaspoon Simple Syrup
1 Egg White

Combine ingredients in a mixing glass filled with cracked ice. Shake vigorously, and strain into a cocktail coupe glass.

Bee's Knees

Frank Meier became the best-known drink shaker in the world. He might not have merited that distinction before Prohibition, but after passage of the Volstead Act, all wet lanes led to Paris. The noted concocter behind the bar of the Ritz Hotel devised the easy-drinking Bee's Knees, a cocktail that took Europe—and eventually America—by storm.

1½ ounces Gin
1 teaspoon Honey
Juice of ¼ Lemon

Combine ingredients in a mixing glass filled with cracked ice. Shake vigorously, and strain into a cocktail coupe glass.

The Communist

Communism is identified with the color red for "blood of the workers," inspiring a vintage cocktail formula that first appeared in a 1933 cocktail pamphlet called *Cocktail Parade*. Ingredients in the red-hued cocktail add up to a full, fresh restorative, shaken until as cold as Mother Russia. Sweet and savory black cherry essence mingles easily with citrus juices, building a bridge to the herbal notes of gin. To your health, comrade!

1 ounce Gin
1 ounce Orange Juice, freshly squeezed
¾ ounce Lemon Juice, freshly squeezed
½ ounce Cherry Heering

Combine ingredients in a mixing glass filled with cracked ice. Shake vigorously, and strain into a cocktail coupe glass.

20th Century

A cocktail composed in 1937 by a British bartender named C. A. Tuck and bestowed in honor of the Twentieth Century Limited, the express passenger train which ran between Grand Central Terminal in New York City and LaSalle Street Station in Chicago. The recipe was first published in 1937 in the *Café Royal Cocktail Book* by William J. Tarling, president of the United Kingdom Bartenders' Guild and head bartender at London's Café Royal.

1½ ounces Gin
¾ ounce Kina Lillet
¾ ounce White Crème de Cacao
¾ ounce Lemon Juice, freshly squeezed
Lemon peel, for garnish

Combine ingredients in a mixing glass filled with cracked ice. Shake vigorously, and strain into a cocktail coupe glass. Express lemon peel over the glass, rub it around the rim, and drop it in.

Between the Sheets

Johnny Brooks, a bartender who practiced his art at the Stork Club, the '21' Club, the Waldorf-Astoria, and the Beachcomber during a noteworthy career, invented this member of the sour family at the Seven Seas in New Rochelle, New York. His recipe is a variation on the Sidecar, but instead cleverly adds rum to equal measures of brandy and Cointreau.

¾ ounce Brandy
¾ ounce Cointreau
¾ ounce Rum

Juice of ½ Lemon
Lemon peel, for garnish

Combine ingredients in a mixing glass filled with cracked ice. Shake vigorously, and strain into a cocktail coupe glass. Express lemon peel over the glass, rub it around the rim, and drop it in.

The Bellamy Scotch Sour

"The Stork Club symbolizes and epitomizes the deluxe upholstery of quintessentially urban existence," writes Lucius Beebe in *The Stork Club Bar Book*. Regarding head barman Nathaniel "Cookie" Cook and the cocktail devised by a well-known actor, Beebe writes, "Cookie may prescribe for the drooping customer a very special pick-me-up, dreamed up in a bemused moment by Ralph Bellamy. This, says Mr. Bellamy, in a triumph of understatement, is a drink for lazy Sunday afternoons and requires no superselling."

1½ ounces Orange Juice, freshly squeezed
1 ounce Lemon Juice, freshly squeezed
3 ounces Scotch Whisky

½ teaspoon Honey
1 dash Angostura Bitters
1 piece preserved Ginger, for garnish

Frappé liquid ingredients until freezing cold in a blender, pour into a cocktail coupe glass, and garnish with ginger on a stick.

Eastern Sour

Victor Bergeron, owner and master mixologist of a chain of South Seas-inspired restaurants that bore his nickname, "Trader Vic," originated the Eastern Sour sometime in the 1950s, its name a reference to the East Indies. A more exotic riff on the sour cocktail with bourbon as the base spirit, later variations included the London Sour made with Scotch instead of bourbon and a Munich Sour soaked with brandy.

2 ounces Bourbon
½ ounce Orange Juice, freshly squeezed
½ ounce Lemon Juice, freshly squeezed

1 dash Orgeat Syrup
1 dash Simple Syrup
Lime peel, for garnish

Combine ingredients in a mixing glass filled with cracked ice. Shake vigorously, and strain into a double Old Fashioned glass filled with ice. Express lime peel over the glass, rub it around the rim, and drop it in.

Long Island Iced Tea

It was once described as the most popular summer singles bar on the East Coast. In 1972, Robert "Rosebud" Butt, a bartender at the Oak Beach Inn (the OBI), a nightclub in Babylon, Long Island, mixed four different spirits to create one powerful drink. At first it was just called "Iced Tea," with "Long Island" added to the name when the drink caught on around the country.

1 ounce Vodka
1 ounce Gin
1 ounce Rum
1 ounce Tequila
½ ounce Triple Sec

¾ ounce Lemon Juice, freshly squeezed
¾ ounce Simple Syrup
1 splash Coca Cola, or to taste
2 Lemon wedges

Build a highball or hurricane glass with ice, and add all the ingredients except the cola. Top with a splash of cola, and stir briefly. Garnish with lemon wedges. Serve with straw.

Penicillin

Time magazine called it the "transmogrification of a whiskey sour." A modern classic devised by New York bartender Sammy Ross of New York's Milk & Honey, this curative cocktail includes warming, soothing flavors of honey, lemon juice, and fresh ginger, fortified with a dose of Scotch and a touch of single malt for a comforting hint of "smoky peat."

2 ounces Scotch
¾ ounce Lemon Juice, freshly squeezed
¾ ounce Honey-Ginger Syrup*

1 dash Single Malt Scotch
Candied Ginger, for garnish

combine bourbon, lemon juice, and syrup in a mixing glass filled with cracked ice. Shake vigorously, and strain into a rocks glass filled with fresh ice. Garnish with a piece of candied ginger.

*Honey-Ginger Syrup: Stir together 1½ ounces honey, 2 tablespoons sugar and ½ ounce water in a small bowl. Run 1 large piece of fresh ginger through a juicer—or grate finely—and squeeze in a piece of cheesecloth to separate the juice. Add 1½ ounces of ginger juice, and stir until the sugar and honey dissolve.

New York Sour

Cocktails have come and gone and come back again. At Founding Farmers in Washington, DC, Beverage Director Jon Arroyo revives a wine-spiked whiskey sour with new vigor (a version of the New York Sour first appeared in Harry Craddock's *Savoy Cocktail Book*). According to Mr. Arroyo, a perfectly balanced sour is a work of art, and this drink provides a perfect balance of sour citrus and soft sweetness, sipped through the layer of a jammy red wine.

2 ounces Buffalo Trace Bourbon
¾ ounce Lemon Juice, freshly squeezed

¾ ounce Simple Syrup
½ ounce Merlot (or Rioja)

Combine bourbon, lemon juice, and syrup in a mixing glass filled with cracked ice. Shake vigorously, and strain into a rocks glass filled with fresh ice. Gently pour the wine over the back of a spoon held just above the drink's surface so it floats on top.

Spitfire

At London's 69 Colebrooke Row, mixologist Tony Conigliaro conjures up "summer-in-a-glass," matching a cognac sour with peach liqueur and coaxing out the fruity elements present in cognac. He adds white wine, purposely choosing a Trebbiano, made from the same grape used in the production of cognac, one which expresses slight peachy notes. What he achieves is a harmony of flavors where the sweet stone fruit acts as a bridge between all the ingredients.

1½ ounces Cognac
¾ ounce Lemon Juice, freshly squeezed
¾ ounce Egg White
½ ounce Simple Syrup

½ ounce Crème de Pêche
¾ ounce Trebbiano (or other fruity dry white wine)

Combine the cognac, lemon juice, egg white, simple syrup, and peach liqueur in a mixing glass. Dry shake to emulsify egg. Add cracked ice, and shake again. Strain into a large, chilled cocktail coupe glass, and pour in the dry white wine last.

Paradisi Sour

Sours can be made with any citrus, and Andrew Sienkiewicz of The Last Word in Ann Arbor, Michigan, demonstrates that grapefruit (*Citrus paradisi*) juice pairs exceptionally well with bourbon. The drink is inspired by the vintage Brown Derby cocktail, named after the hat-shaped Los Angeles diner. According to the mixologist, "the simple [syrup] and lemon are optional when grapefruit is in seasonal prime." His reverse double-shake creates a foam with much larger bubbles.

¾ ounce Buffalo Trace Bourbon
¾ ounce Aperol
¾ ounce Grapefruit Juice, freshly squeezed
¼ ounce Lemon Juice, freshly squeezed

¼ ounce Simple Syrup
1 Egg White
Orange peel, for garnish

Combine ingredients into a shaker. Add ice, and shake. Strain ice, and discard. Shake ingredients without ice, pour into a double Old Fashioned glass with 3 large cubes. Express orange peel over the glass, rub it around the rim, and rest on top of the foam.

The Colony

The French poet Victor Hugo once wrote, "Life is a flower for which love is the honey." This modification of the vintage, honey-sweetened Bee's Knees from the JCT Kitchen and Bar in Atlanta ramps up tang and backbone when compared to the original with the vinegar reduction's unique acidity.

2 ounces Barr Hill Barrel-Aged Gin
¾ ounce Spiced Honey Gastrique*
½ ounce Lemon Juice, freshly squeezed
1 pinch Fennel Pollen, for garnish

Combine liquid ingredients in a mixing glass with cracked ice. Shake vigorously, and double-strain into a cocktail coupe glass. Garnish with fennel pollen.

*Spiced Honey Gastrique: Liquify 2 cups of honey in a small sauce pan over medium heat. Add ½ cup of Champagne vinaigrette, and stir to combine. Once the mixture begins to caramelize, remove from heat, and allow to cool. Add a pinch of salt and 1 tablespoon of black pepper. Stir to combine. Refrigerate for up to 2 weeks.

∙∙

Art Nouveau

François Vera leads a team of mixologists at Pour Vous, a Parisian-themed lounge in Hollywood, California. The romantic aesthetic serves as inspiration for Mr. Vera's modern take on the Champs-Élysées cocktail, a sophisticated cousin of the Sidecar listed in the 1930 *Savoy Cocktail Book*. Take a seat on one of the red velvet tufted banquettes to sip an artful combination of Armagnac and absinthe, citrus and sweet.

1½ ounces Armagnac
½ ounce Absinthe
½ ounce Lemon Juice, freshly squeezed

½ ounce Simple Syrup
Lemon peel, for garnish

Combine ingredients in a mixing glass with cracked ice. Shake vigorously, and strain into chilled cocktail coupe glass. Express lemon peel over the glass, rub it around the rim, and drop it in.

Pepperbox

The Prohibition-era Last Word cocktail, developed at the Detroit Athletic Club during the 1920s, provides inspiration for a gin-forward revision at the Red Feather Lounge in Boise, Idaho. The taste varies slightly depending on the brand of gin being used: Plymouth provides fresh juniper and lemony bite. The palate is at once a little sour, a little sweet, and a little pungent.

2 ounces Plymouth Gin
½ ounce Green Chartreuse
½ ounce Lime Juice, freshly squeezed

Splash of Simple Syrup, to taste
Candied Lemon, for garnish
Freshly ground Pepper, for garnish

Combine ingredients in a mixing glass with cracked ice. Shake vigorously, and strain into chilled cocktail coupe glass. Grind fresh pepper onto a candied lemon, and drop on the surface of the drink.

Little Osaka Sour

Sawtelle Boulevard in Los Angeles, from Santa Monica Boulevard to Olympic Boulevard, is called "Little Osaka," home to Plan Check Kitchen + Bar, where the twist on a traditional whiskey sour reflects the city's Japanese neighborhood. An impish nuance of fruity plum essence provides course correction in a cocktail that stands up to the umami in Chef Uchimura's dishes.

2 ounces Buffalo Trace Bourbon
1 ounce Lemon Juice, freshly squeezed
¾ ounce Simple Syrup

1 Egg White
¼ ounce Fu-ki Plum Wine
2 dashes Angostura Bitters

Combine bourbon, lemon juice, simple syrup, and egg white in a mixing glass. Dry shake for about 20 seconds. Add cracked ice to mixing glass and shake. Strain into a rocks glass over fresh ice. Float plum wine over the top, and garnish with bitters.

Ignacio Sour

The variations for a sour are almost endless. At the Harbord Room in Toronto, mixologist Dave Mitton orchestrates a potent combination of diverse elements—an enchantingly smoky interpretation named for Ignacio Ortiz, director of the film *Mezcal*. The sharp bite of the Mexican spirit is fleshed out with a little Bénédictine, almond sweetener, and lemon citrus.

1 Egg White
1½ ounces Fortuna Mezcal
½ ounce Bénédictine
¾ ounce Lemon Juice, freshly squeezed

½ ounce Orgeat Syrup
Orange peel, for garnish
Grated Nutmeg, for garnish

Dry shake the egg white in shaker to emulsify, about 7–8 seconds. Add remaining ingredients and dry shake for an additional 5–6 seconds. Add cracked ice, and shake again. Fine-strain into a cocktail glass with new ice. Express orange peel over the glass, rub it around the rim, drop it in, then lightly dust with nutmeg over the top.

Long Iceland Iced Tea

Cocktail gurus at The Goat in London strip away the stereotype to concoct a cheeky, sweet-tart libation, inspired by a notion of the Long Island classic, borrowing influences of peach from the classic Bellini cocktail and dressing up with quintessentially British Earl Grey tea.

1½ ounces Earl Grey Tea–Infused Reyka
   Icelandic Vodka*
1½ ounces White Peach Purée
3 dashes Fee Brothers Peach Bitters

Juice of ½ Lemon
½ ounce Monin Honey Syrup
Loose leaf Earl Grey Tea, for garnish

Add ingredients to a mixing glass with ice. Shake vigorously, and strain over new ice in a margarita glass. Cap with crushed ice, and garnish with a light sprinkle of loose leaf Earl Grey tea.

*Earl Grey Tea–Infused Reyka Icelandic Vodka: Using a funnel, place 6 level teaspoons of Earl Grey tea leaves into a 750 ml bottle of the vodka. Replace the cap of the bottle, and shake well. Steep overnight. Pour the mixture through a strainer, and funnel into a clean bottle. Discard the tea leaves.

Oliveto

This cross between a gin sour and a Ramos fizz is the handiwork of mixologist Pip Hanson at the Marvel Bar in Minneapolis, Minnesota, who describes his interpretation as "an emulsified sour, a drink that uses egg white to emulsify olive oil into the mix." The egg foam combines with the oil to provide a soft, silky meringue texture on the tongue, and since olive oil is the hallmark ingredient, it should be a high quality, full-bodied oil.

2 ounces Gin
¾ ounce Lemon Juice, freshly squeezed
⅓ ounce Licor 43
⅓ ounce Simple Syrup

1 Egg White
½ ounce Extra-Virgin Olive Oil
3 large Ice Cubes

Combine ingredients in a mixing glass, and shake vigorously until you can hear that the ice has almost melted away, about 2 minutes. Strain into a stemless wine glass.

Chinese Exchange Student

In northern China it's customary to serve jasmine tea as a welcoming gesture to guests. With that in mind, Ollie Riley of Tom Brown's Brasserie in Nottingham, England, perfumes a reception raspberry sour with the intoxicating fragrance of jasmine tea, properly served not in a cocktail glass but in a porcelain teacup.

1½ ounces Absolut Rasberri
½ ounce Briottet Crème de Framboise
1½ ounces Jasmine Tea
½ ounce Lemon Juice, freshly squeezed

½ ounce Simple Syrup
3 fresh Raspberries, for garnish
Jasmine Tea leaves, for garnish

Brew jasmine tea to ensure a strong cup (add 3 or 4 times as much tea as a normal cup of tea). Leave to brew and cool. Fine strain the tea to get rid of excess tea leaves. Combine ingredients in a mixing glass with cracked ice, and stir gently until well-mixed and chilled. Strain into tea cup with saucer. Garnish with raspberries and tea leaves on the saucer.

The Burlesque

Mixologist Sean McKenzie of the Guild Tavern in South Burlington, Vermont, pays an interpretive nod to a classic cocktail of New Orleans, marking a bright red stripe over the top. Liberating Bénédictine adds virility to the lively, honey-sweetened rye sour, while absinthe adds complexity as a third or fourth note. It's an ambiguous mix yet a strict example of citrus and sweetness in harmony.

2 ounces Old Overholt Rye Whiskey
¾ ounce Lemon Juice, freshly squeezed
½ ounce Bénédictine
½ ounce Honey Syrup*

1 teaspoon Lucid Absinthe
1 Egg White
2 dashes Fee Brothers Cranberry Bitters

Combine all ingredients except bitters. Dry shake to emulsify egg. Add cracked ice, and shake again. Double-strain into a cocktail coupe glass. Garnish with line of bitters on top of the foam.

*Honey Syrup: Combine 1 cup honey and 1 cup water in a small saucepan over medium heat, and stir until fully incorporated. Remove from heat, let cool to room temperature, and transfer to a clean glass jar. Cover, and keep refrigerated for up to 2 weeks.

The St. Aperol

Jack Nolan of Fortify Kitchen and Bar in Clayton, Georgia, hews closely to the contours and sensibility of a vodka sour, then combines two apéritifs, St. Germain and Aperol to season the drink and whet the appetite. Absolut Vodka blends perfectly in a supple, feather-soft drink.

1½ ounces Absolut Vodka
¾ ounce St. Germain Elderflower Liqueur
½ ounce Aperol

¾ ounce Lemon Juice, freshly squeezed
½ ounce Simple Syrup
Orange wheel, for garnish

Combine ingredients in a mixing glass filled with cracked ice. Shake vigorously, and strain into a chilled cocktail coupe glass. Float orange wheel over the top.

Yuzu Clover Club

Wes Morgan, mixologist at China Doll in Sydney, Australia, puts a Far Eastern spin on the vintage Clover Club cocktail, counterbalancing citrus with sweet, jewel-toned raspberry syrup, and sharing the role of gin with Japanese sake, infused with yuzu, a native citrus fruit with notes of lemon, lime and orange.

1 ounce Lemon Juice, freshly squeezed
½ ounce Raspberry Syrup*
1 ounce Beefeater Gin

1 ounce Ume No Yado Yuzu Sake
1 dash Egg White
3 freeze-dried Raspberries, for garnish

Add all ingredients into mixing glass. Dry shake without ice, then shake with ice. Double-strain into chilled Martini glass, and garnish with 3 freeze-dried raspberries.

*Raspberry Syrup: Stir 1 cup of sugar and 1 cup of water over low heat until sugar has dissolved. Add 1 cup of raspberries (fresh or frozen), stirring until the berries form a pulp. Strain into a jar, and refrigerate.

Daddy Issues

Bar director David Shenaut of Portland, Oregon's Raven & Rose glances back at both the White Lady and Bee's Knees as template for an expressive approach to the vodka sour. A liqueur from the Loire Valley adds fragrance of ripe peaches to the virtuosic blend of sweet and tart.

1 ounce New Deal Hot Monkey Vodka
¾ ounce Combier Crème de Pêche de Vigne
¾ ounce Lemon Juice, freshly squeezed
½ ounce Honey

1 teaspoon Bénédictine
1 Egg White
Angostura Bitters, for garnish

Combine liquid ingredients in a cocktail shaker without ice. Add egg white to shaker, close, and dry shake for about 20 seconds to thoroughly emulsify. Add cracked ice, and shake vigorously again. Strain into a chilled cocktail coupe glass. Layer a couple drops of bitters onto the foam, and swirl with a cocktail pick to decorate.

Dark Passenger

Harkening back to a time when bars were bastions of civility and sophistication, Cure introduces New Orleanians to proprietary libations like the Dark Passenger, a variation on the Sidecar created by mixologist Genevieve Mashburn. It's crafted with an eccentric Madeira, grappa infused with bitter almond, and Premier Cru de Cognac (modeled on a vintage spirit that bartending pioneers of the nineteenth century would have used for their juleps, Crustas and punches), a union of the convergent and the divergent.

1½ ounces Rare Wine Company "Savannah" Verdelho Madeira
¾ ounce Pierre Ferrand "1840 Original Formula" Grande Champagne Cognac
¾ ounce Lemon Juice, freshly squeezed

½ ounce Nardini Mandorla Almond Grappa
¼ ounce Turbinado Simple Syrup
14 drops Haas Brothers Amargo Vallet
Lemon peel, to express

Combine ingredients in a mixing glass with minimal ice (2 or 3 cubes). Shake briefly but vigorously, and double-strain into a chilled cocktail coupe glass. Express lemon peel over the glass, then discard.

Howard Hawks

Mixologist Jeremy Lake of the Lost Property Bar, located at the historic Los Angeles corner of Hollywood and Vine, dedicates his interpretation of the classic Morning Glory Fizz to chameleonic director Howard Hawks, a craftsman who made tight, lean pictures during the studio era. (Hawks was a drinking partner of William Faulkner and Ernest Hemingway).

1 Egg White
⅜ ounce Lemon Juice, freshly squeezed
⅜ ounce Lime Juice, freshly squeezed
¾ ounce Simple Syrup
1 ounce Old Overholt Rye Whiskey

1 ounce Stolen "Coffee & Cigarettes" Spiced Rum
1 dash Absinthe
3 Coffee Beans, for garnish

Combine liquid ingredients (except absinthe) in a cocktail shaker without ice, and dry shake for about 20 seconds to thoroughly emulsify the egg white. Add cracked ice, and shake vigorously again. Rinse a rocks glass with the absinthe, making sure to coat the entire inside of the glass. Double-strain into the prepared glass. Garnish with coffee beans.

White Rabbit

Alice in Wonderland's White Rabbit is the surprising and interesting character Alice follows that leads to all her adventures. At the Whippoorwill in Toronto, Tyler Newsome's appealing base spirit—a pot still whiskey—is the most interesting character, adding rich, complex flavors to his whiskey sour composition. Citrus is just present enough to balance the sweetness of the honey syrup.

1¾ ounces Jameson Select Reserve
   Black Barrel
1 ounce Lemon Juice, freshly squeezed

¾ ounce Peppered Honey Syrup*
5 drops Bitterman's Hopped Grapefruit Bitters
½ ounce Egg White

Combine ingredients in a mixing glass. Close the shaker, and dry shake for about 20 seconds to thoroughly emulsify the egg white. Add cracked ice, and shake vigorously again. Double strain into a cocktail coupe glass.

*Peppered Honey Syrup: Heat 1 teaspoon black peppercorns in a skillet over medium heat until smoking. Remove from heat, and add to ½ cup honey and ½ cup water. Stir to combine. Allow 2 days for flavors to infuse. Strain out peppercorns.

The Silver Spoon

Mixologist Chad Walsh lightens things up at The Dutch in New York City with Dobel Silver—a blend of *reposado* and *añejo* tequilas, aged in European white oak barrels, then filtered to remove all color—as his primary ingredient. A splash of soda makes the drink a fizz variation on the vintage sours family of cocktails.

1½ ounces Maestro Dobel Silver Tequila
¾ ounce Peychaud's Bitters
¼ ounce Luxardo Maraschino
¾ ounce Lemon Juice, freshly squeezed

½ ounce Simple Syrup
1 Egg White
Club Soda, chilled
3 Maraschino Cherries, for garnish

Combine ingredients (except soda) in a mixing glass. Dry shake, then shake with cracked ice. Strain into a Collins glass, and top up with soda. Garnish with 3 maraschino cherries.

INDEX

ACKNOWLEDGMENTS

The authors wish to thank all those who contributed original cocktail recipes and informed expertise. These practitioners of the mixologist's art represent many of the most progressive beverage programs in the world. Without their skill, wisdom, and generosity, this book would not have happened.

The authors would also like to thank the following photographers for their efforts:

Carly Diaz (Manhattan Nouveau)
Meredith Perdue (In Cold Blood)
Ken Fletcher (White Star)
Robert Donovan (The Carpetbagger)
Miguel Emmanuelli (Blonde Negroni)

Special gratitude to Chamois Holschuh and the entire team of professionals at Skyhorse Publishing, for the confidence, enthusiasm, and support they gave us.

—Julia and Michael

ABOUT THE AUTHORS

Julia Hastings-Black has been working her way around the food world for more than a decade. As a cook, gardener, recipe tester, cooking instructor, and researcher in the history of food writing, she is fascinated by the intersection of food and language.

For nearly three decades, Michael Turback combined inventiveness, passionate cooking with local ingredients, and an award-winning list of regional wines at his legendary Ithaca, New York restaurant. As an author, he has previously taken on, with distinction, such single topics as the ice cream sundae, the banana split, hot chocolate, mocha, coffee drinks, and progressive gin cocktails. He has authored cookbooks for the Ithaca Farmers Market and the historic North Market in Columbus, Ohio. His annually updated *Finger Lakes Uncorked* is considered the definitive guide to Upstate New York wine country.

In *Cocktails at Dinner*, their first collaboration for Skyhorse Publishing, Julia and Michael explore the mutual attraction of cocktails and food with an imaginative collection of companionable recipes.